Albania

Neil Olsen

Oxfam

First published by Oxfam GB in 2000

ISBN 0 85598 432 5

A catalogue record for this publication is available from the British Library.

Available from the following agents:

USA: Stylus Publishing LLC,
PO Box 605, Herndon, VA 20172-0605, USA
tel: +1 (0)703 661 1581; fax: + 1(0)703 661 1547;
email: styluspub@aol.com; website www.styluspub.com

Canada: Fernwood Books Ltd,
PO Box 9409, Stn. 'A', Halifax, N.S. B3K 5S3, Canada
tel: +1 (0)902 422 3302; fax: +1 (0)902 422 3179;
e-mail: fernwood@istar.ca

India: Maya Publishers Pvt Ltd,
113-B, Shapur Jat, New Delhi-110049, India
tel: +91 (0)11 649 4850; fax: +91 (0)11 649 1039;
email: surit@del2.vsnl.net.in

K Krishnamurthy,
23 Thanikachalan Road, Madras 600017, India
tel: +91 (0)44 434 4519; fax: +91 (0)44 434 2009;
email: ksm@md2.vsnl.net.in

South Africa, Zimbabwe, Botswana, Lesotho, Namibia, Swaziland:
David Philip Publishers,
PO Box 23408, Claremont 7735, South Africa
tel: +27 (0)21 64 4136; fax: +27(0)21 64 3358;
email: dppsales@iafrica.com

Tanzania: Mkuki na Nyota Publishers,
PO Box 4246, Dar es Salaam, Tanzania
tel/fax: +255 (0)51 180479, email: mkuki@ud.co.tz

Australia: Bush Books,
PO Box 1958, Gosford, NSW 2250, Australia
tel: +61 (0)2 043 233 274; fax: +61 (0)2 092 122 468,
email: bushbook@ozemail.com.au

Rest of the world: contact Oxfam Publishing,
274 Banbury Road, Oxford OX2 7DZ, UK.
tel. +44 (0)1865 311 311; fax +44 (0)1865 313 925;
email publish@oxfam.org.uk;
website www.oxfam.org.uk/publications.html

Printed by
Information Press, Southfield Road, Eynsham OX8 1JJ, UK

Published by
Oxfam GB, 274 Banbury Road, Oxford OX2 7DZ, UK

Series designed by
Richard Morris, Stonesfield Design.
This title designed by Rowie Christopher Design.
Typeset in FF Scala and Gill Sans.

Cover designed by
Rowie Christopher

Oxfam GB is a registered charity, no. 202 918, and is a member of Oxfam International.

Photo acknowledgements:

All photographs © Rhodri Jones for Oxfam GB, except as follows:

Bonita Glanville-Morris (©Oxfam GB): 36 bottom

Jenny Matthews (© Oxfam GB): 8

Douglas Saltmarshe (©Oxfam GB): 65

AKG London: 17 box

Arben Bregu: 28/29

Hardlines: 11

Jim Rees: 15

Contents

Introduction: freedom at last	5
The country and its people	12
History: from Skenderbeg to Hoxha	17
The painful transition to democracy	23
The legacy of central planning	30
In search of a living: the lure of Europe	37
Education: changing needs and ideas	42
The health system under pressure	47
New concepts and freedoms	52
Albanian women's struggle for equality	55
Unlocking the doors: the challenges facing people with disabilities	60
The environment: too little, too late?	65
'Europe's wild west': the breakdown of law and order	70
Albanian identity and the Balkan factor	74
Conclusion: the need for choice and opportunity	79
Dates and events	82
Facts and figures	84
Sources and further reading	85
Oxfam in Albania	86
Index	87

▲ A bird's eye view of Skenderbeg Square; people are gathering for a political rally in 1992.

► The mural over the entrance to the National Museum.

Introduction: freedom at last

Most outsiders' first and lasting impression of Albania is of Skenderbeg Square in the heart of Tiranë, the nation's capital. The buildings that surround this square reflect the country's turbulent and fascinating history: from Ottoman bureaucracy to Italian occupation, from austere communism to rollercoaster capitalism. Framed by the impressive grandeur of Mount Dajti, the imposing statue of Skenderbeg—the country's mediaeval founder and first national hero—stands proudly in the centre of the square. Ranged around the statue are a mosque dating from the sixteenth century, the impressive but crumbling Opera House built by the Communists, and the new Tiranë International Hotel where Europe comes to make deals with this new free-market economy. Turning around the square, you see the imposing National Museum with its giant mural, built to commemorate the 'great people's struggle' and establishment of the Communist state in 1944. A huge statue of Enver Hoxha which used to stand next to the Museum was toppled by rioting students in December 1990; until recently its space was occupied by Ferris wheels, amusement rides, and other tokens of the new consumer state. Turning full circle, you see grandiose buildings erected during the Italian occupation in the Second World War, which have continued to serve as government buildings to this day.

The square itself is a chaotic mix of dilapidated cars roaring around at breakneck speed; death-defying cyclists and pedestrians weaving their way between desperate drivers; old women in colourful traditional costumes, who come from the rural areas in donkey carts to sell their produce and buy supplies at the market; and old men wearing the traditional white crushed-felt hats of the mountains.

► *The statue of Gjergj Skenderbeg in the square that is named after him. While many communist icons were destroyed during the 1990s, symbols of national pride were left untouched.*

Well-dressed, energetic younger people hustle by, stopping to chat to friends. The air is thick with the smell of diesel and fried food from the many stands selling *Qofte* and *Byrek*, traditional meat and filo pastry snacks.

At the end of your tour around Skenderbeg Square, you are left with an impression of a country in a desperate hurry to get somewhere, but not quite sure where that 'somewhere' is. Albania is a country of enormous energy and excitement, although—as this book tries to show—there is still a need to deal with the past and embrace the future in a way that has meaning for all Albanians. The endurance of Albanians is being put to the test as the country struggles to break free of its past and make sense of its new-found freedom. The events of 1990 and 1991 and the transition to 'democracy' have had dramatic effects, both positive and negative, on all Albanians. The new sense of freedom has a different meaning to each of them, as their stories and accounts in this book will show.

The legacy of foreign domination

At the end of 1990 and during the early months of 1991, Albania began its struggle to free itself from 50 years of communist oppression. Albania was the last country to be caught in the tidal wave of communist collapse in Eastern and Central Europe that began in the late 1980s. Albania's transformation was also to be the most painful and traumatic for its people, as they have struggled to embrace democracy and freedom while trying to dismantle the oppression of one of the world's last surviving Stalinist states.

Albanians have had very little say in their own destiny for the past 600 years. In the fourteenth century, the country fell under the control of the Ottoman Empire, and later became the European powers' playground in their long campaign to rid Europe of Turkish influence. From 1500 to 1944, Albania enjoyed only 18 years of genuine sovereignty, and although the country regained its independence in 1944, its citizens were denied even the most basic of freedoms by Enver Hoxha's oppressive, isolationist communist government. For the next 47 years, Albanians had very little chance to participate in shaping their country, and with the constant threat of political persecution, their priorities became simply to avoid suspicion and survive. Although by late 1990 Albanians took to the streets to overthrow

▲ *Vjosë River seen from the mountains between Gjirokastër and Tepelenë.*

the communist regime, the advent of democracy in 1992 has not changed their ability to participate fully in building a new society.

This legacy of foreign domination of Albanian affairs, and the isolation and repression of the communist years, have left Albanians ill equipped to establish a truly democratic and equitable society. It will be difficult for the concept of 'civil society' to take root in a society whose members have not been encouraged to work together, except under threat of imprisonment or execution. Furthermore, tribal traditions and suspicion of outsiders, even from village to village, serve to negate what little sense of community and co-operation has survived. The Albanian word for 'foreigner' refers not just to people from outside the country, but even to people from other villages. In Albania—as in many other countries—allegiances are first and foremost to the family, rather than to a community, and this will take a long time to change.

The recent upheavals in Kosovo

European powers drew up modern-day Albania's borders in 1912, without significant consultation with Albanians; a process which left almost 3 million Albanians as second-class citizens in neighbouring countries. Since the initial research for this book, the lives of thousands of ethnic Albanians in the Serbian province of Kosovo have been turned upside down. Even before a rising number of atrocities forced Kosovar Albanians to flee their homes and take to the mountains in January 1999, Albania was host to between 10,000 and 15,000 Kosovar refugees fleeing systematic persecution and intimidation from Serb forces. Two-thirds of these refugees found accommodation with Albanian families. At the height of the NATO airstrikes that began in March of 1999 — which prompted about 800,000 Kosovar Albanians to seek refuge from intensified Serb attacks in neighbouring countries — Albania hosted up to 500,000 refugees. Struggling with a lack of infrastructure to support such a refugee influx, Albania has shown to the world that its people are capable of extraordinary compassion and generosity, even in the face of severe economic hardship and fears for the security of their own country. But it must be remembered that it is the country in the Balkans that can least afford such generosity.

▼ *A family of Kosovar Albanians in the refugee camp near Kukës in 1999.*

With the end of the military conflict in the summer of 1999, and the installation of a NATO-led international peacekeeping force in Kosovo, most of the refugees returned home, despite the fact that their homes had been looted and their livelihoods destroyed by the departing Serbian forces. A retaliatory campaign of intimidation against those Serbs who remain in Kosovo is now being carried out by the Kosovo Liberation Army (KLA) and the Albanian mafia. Power struggles between the KLA and the former underground government of the Democratic League of Kosovo are worrying indicators of future stability, and the prospect of further conflict has direct implications for events in Albania.

Leaving the past behind

As a result of the past ten years' turmoil in the Balkans, Albania has been thrust onto the world stage. It is making efforts to become a modern, democratic state, ultimately eligible for entry into the European Union, but it has had very little time to prepare for this process. Albania's political leaders have simply changed their political colours to suit the expectations of Western, especially European, governments in order to secure desperately needed financial assistance. It is debatable where much of this aid has gone: identifying its effects in Albania today is difficult. For this the West must bear some responsibility, as it must for its manipulation of Albania's fate

◄ A communist memorial, now a place where the old and the new coexist.

in the late nineteenth and early twentieth century. In the period since 1990, the political and strategic concerns of Western governments for security in the Balkans have skewed the pattern of Albania's recent development. Desperate to avoid floods of Albanian economic refugees (as witnessed in 1991) and a further spread of the Balkan conflicts, Western and European governments have been willing to pay a high price for security in Albania. In the interests of Balkan security and containment, they turned a blind eye to much of the corruption and authoritarianism of the country's first post-communist government. As for most of this century, ordinary Albanians have had very little opportunity to play a part in shaping a new reality for their country since overthrowing the communist regime in 1990–91.

As a result, most Albanians continue to be suspicious of government, and increasingly rely on developing their own solutions to the problems of injustice and inequality in their country. Such solutions have often been rooted in the hatred and frustration emanating from the previous 50 years of oppression. In 1997, the world watched in horror as scenes of gun-toting Albanian teenagers filled their television screens—without trying to understand the enormous pressures Albanian society has been under since 1990. With its economy in ruins and as a nervous witness to the break-up of Yugoslavia, Albania has faced great difficulties in trying to establish any kind of stability. In such a volatile environment, Albanians have found it hard to plan for the future with any degree of confidence. The violent events of 1997 have left people with no faith whatsoever in the state or political institutions. This is made worse by the continued lack of economic and physical security as well as by concern about the situation in Kosovo.

The people of Europe's poorest country, which foreign media often simplistically liken to 'Europe's Wild West', are struggling to make sense of the chaos and uncertainty of the past eight years. For most Albanians,

▼ A stereotypical image, but for many Albanian teenagers it is normal to have small arms around the house.

▲ *The giant mausoleum in Tiranë, which Hoxha built for himself during his lifetime, is now in use as a conference centre.*

the struggle for daily survival is their primary concern, and as a result, it is almost impossible for them to think long-term about their future. Because of these difficulties it would be foolish to pretend that Albania is a country bubbling with optimism; indeed, many young people can only think of leaving the country. But none the less, Albania is a beautiful country with some of the most generous and hospitable people in Europe. Albanians are desperate for the world to see another side of their country than the images of decay and chaos so often portrayed in the foreign media. Despite the brutality of their past history, Albanians have managed to retain their dignity, pride, generosity, and even a sense of humour. It is these qualities which the Albanian government and the international community must continue to nurture and support as Albanians strive to put the past behind them, and make a fresh start for themselves and their country.

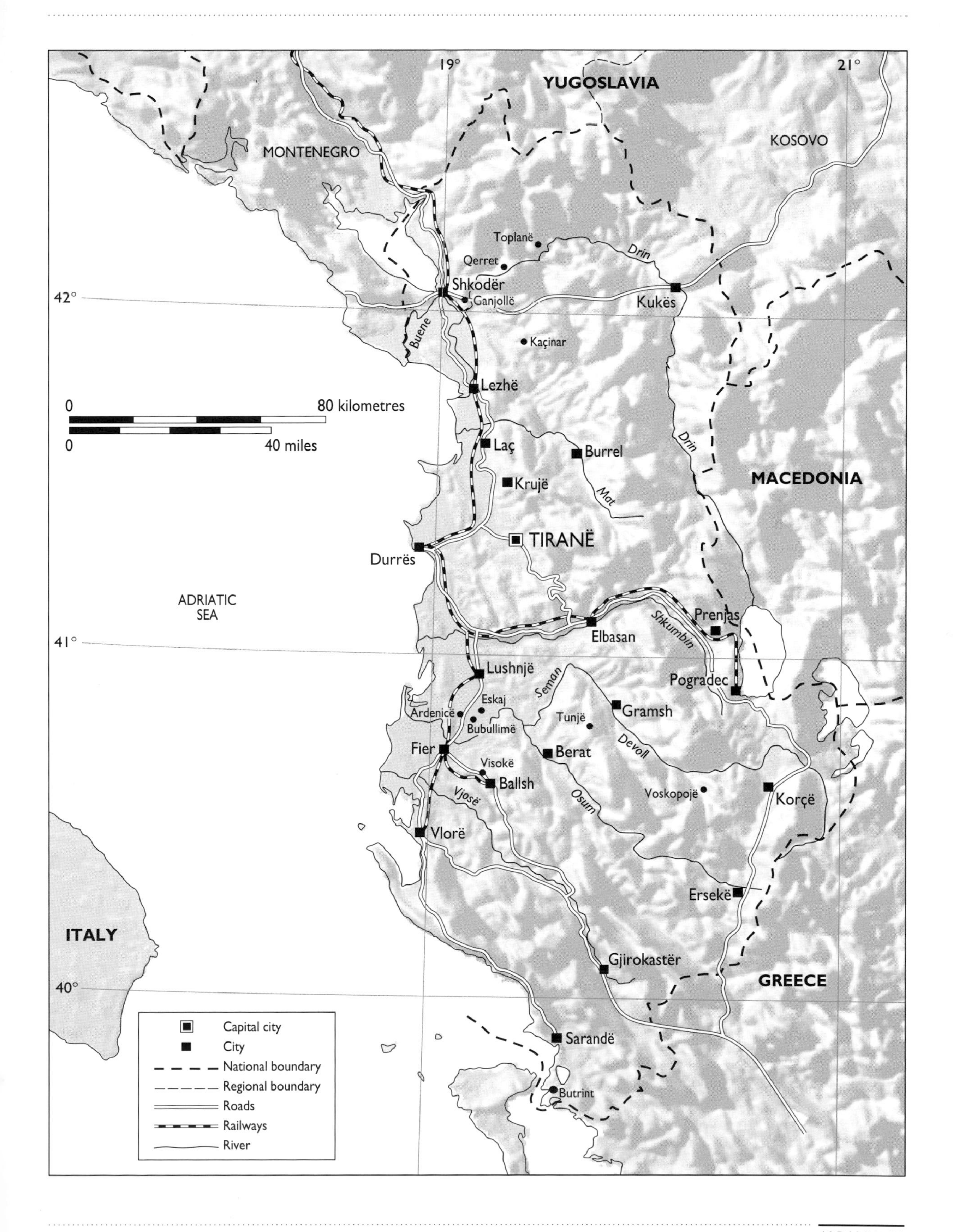
19°
21°
YUGOSLAVIA
MONTENEGRO
KOSOVO
Toplanë
Qerret
Drin
Shkodër
Ganjollë
Kukës
42°
Buene
Kaçinar
Lezhë
0
80 kilometres
0
40 miles
Laç
Burrel
Drin
Krujë
Mat
MACEDONIA
TIRANË
Durrës
ADRIATIC
SEA
Prenjas
Elbasan
Shkumbin
41°
Lushnjë
Seman
Pogradec
Eskaj
Ardenicë
Bubullimë
Tunjë
Gramsh
Fier
Berat
Devoll
Visokë
Ballsh
Vjosë
Osum
Voskopojë
Korçë
Vlorë
Ersekë
ITALY
Gjirokastër
GREECE
40°
Capital city
City
National boundary
Regional boundary
Roads
Railways
River
Sarandë
Butrint

The country and its people

Albania is a small country of 3.5 million people. To the north and northeast lie the Yugoslav Republics of Montenegro and Serbia, whose province of Kosovo shares a border with Albania. The former Yugoslav Republic of Macedonia and Greece lie to the east and the south. The west of Albania is a coastline with beautiful beaches along the Adriatic Sea. Striking mountain ranges predominate the landscape throughout the country, with the exception of the coastal plains where most of Albania's agricultural production takes place. The country's Albanian name *Shqiperi* means 'land of eagles', and one can see why as one travels across numerous rugged ranges throughout the country. Six main rivers and about 150 tributaries flow through the valleys towards the Adriatic Sea, and the northern lakes reflect the stunning mountain landscapes.

Albania's geographical position made it an important point on trade routes between the East and Europe. Because the country was ruled first by the Byzantine Empire, then the Ottoman Empire and later had strong trade links with Italy, the Muslim faith and Christian denominations coexist. The majority of the population is of Muslim origin, 20 per cent are Greek

▼ The mediaeval castle in Gjirokastër, which grew into a city during the 13th century and became an important centre of trade, culture, and politics in southern Albania.

'Albania ... is a country rarely visited ... though abounding in more natural beauties than the classical regions of Greece.'

Lord Byron, letter to Henry Drury, 3 May 1810

▲ Hoxha banned all religious expression in 1967 and tried to create an atheist state, but today Albania enjoys religious freedom and tolerance.

Orthodox, and 10 per cent are Catholic. One notable facet of Albanian society is the extraordinary tolerance with which religion is regarded. Mixed marriages are common, and it is not unusual to see neighbours of different faiths joining in the religious festivities of others. Religion today is not considered a major issue, and although people are now free to worship again—a right denied to them during communism, when Albania was the world's only officially atheist state—there have been no tensions between the different religious groups.

Albania's significance as a trade route in past centuries can still be seen in some of its cities and towns, whose architecture reflects their growth and recalls prosperous times. UNESCO has made the ancient city of Butrint a World Cultural Heritage Site, and Gjirokastër and Berat are also designated. Ancient Greek settlements, such as Apollonia near Vlorë and Orikon south of Fier, are dotted along Albania's coastline.

Albanian is the national language, which is also spoken by ethnic Albanians in Kosovo, Montenegro, and parts of western Macedonia. Albanian is derived from ancient Illyrian and has no similarity with neighbouring Slavic languages or Greek. There are two main dialects which also account for the two main regional cultural differences in Albania: Gheg is spoken in northern Albania, which is typically more rugged and isolated than the south of the country, where Tosk is spoken. (The Greek geographer Strabo already noted this regional division in the first century BC.) Although Albanians feel a sense of kinship with ethnic Albanians in neighbouring countries, divergent historical developments have reinforced divisions, for example by creating stereotypes: Kosovo Albanians used to consider themselves more cosmopolitan and open than the backward, poor Albanians. The separation of Albanians by national borders does figure in Albanian politics: Berisha's election campaign in 1992 played strongly on

▼ A rich variety of cultural influences and geographic location have created a distinct building style in southern and central Albania.

the issue, and he promised to achieve unity by tearing down the 'Balkan Wall' separating Albanians from Albanians. At other times, politicians have been more careful in their stance on Kosovo.

► *A Roma village in the Gjirokastër area.*

▲ *The Roma tradition of placing dolls on houses while they are built to ward off evil spirits is now a widespread practice.*

Ethnic diversity

Albania has two minorities: the Roma and ethnic Greek communities, who are integrated into Albanian society to differing degrees. Although Greek Albanians, who come from southern Albania, have kept some specific cultural practices and are bilingual, their traditions have merged with local Albanian ones, and Greek Albanians do not, on the whole, suffer discrimination. Because it is quite easy for Greek Albanians to emigrate to Greece, some southern villages have been almost deserted. In the case of the Roma minority, who have a more distinct ethnic and cultural—as well as racial—identity, there seems to be a mutual agreement to 'live and let live'. Roma people are stereotyped by Albanian society (they are called 'gypsies') and would find it hard to find work in jobs other than those considered 'typical' Roma (as musicians, artists, and traders). The fact that Roma people tend to live in close-knit communities and that their children do not always attend school but contribute to the family's survival, for example by begging, contributes to stereotyped views. On the other hand, social and cultural prejudice creates a subtle form of discrimination which many Roma may simply choose to avoid by staying among their own community.

National culture

Each province or district of Albania has its own version of the national dress, and music and traditions specific to that area. These are still very much alive today, despite the arrival of MTV and the worst of European television, with regular programmes of traditional music and folklore being broadcast on national television and radio. Albanians have a strong attachment to their culture, traditions, and history, and this helps to maintain their strong sense of identity. Gjirokastër hosts a national folk festival each year, which is broadcast widely. Competing dance troupes show off their skills; singers render old ballads accompanied by the Çiftelia, a string instrument from the north; and women display their colourful gold-embroidered costumes and locally made copper jewellery. There is currently a debate over whether the festival should be hosted by a different region each year, to reflect the diversity of folk culture. Despite a loss of funding for the arts, which were heavily supported during the communist period, both traditional and modern artists continue to produce important works.

Albanians are also prolific storytellers with a great sense of humour. Albanian humorists seem to be the only people able to parody safely the excesses and deficiencies of present and past governments, and as a result they are adored throughout the country. Regular comedy festivals are shown on television, and ratings equal those of televised international

► *The Gjirokastër folk festival was discontinued after the fall of communism, but resumed in 1995.*

Marriage Rites

In Albania's north, marriages were traditionally arranged by the bridegroom's and bride's families. In past centuries, a match could be made as early as a child's birth; a broken promise would lead to family feuds that could run through generations.

A traditional wedding is not a happy occasion for the bride. She is expected to display sadness at leaving her family home, and in most cases, the sadness is heartfelt. Married life represents hard work at home and in the fields, as well as bearing and bringing up children. There is no wedding ceremony as such: the marriage is considered completed after three days, during which the bride's family has received friends, hosted the bridegroom's family for dinner, and paid a return visit to the couple's new home. Nowadays, weddings all over Albania involve a range of civil or religious ceremonies.

football matches. Some Albanians would argue that the country's comedians are a much more effective barometer of public political opinion than the myriad of fiercely politically partisan national newspapers.

Albanian literature

Under Ottoman rule, writing in the Albanian language was suppressed. In the sixteenth and seventeenth centuries, Catholic missionaries were granted permission to produce some religious books, but Albanian writing only began to flourish with the rise of a nationalist movement in the nineteenth century. Writers like Jeronim de Rada and the Frashëri family published patriotic novels and poems, many of which were based on folk epics and ballads, and historical tales. The period from 1878 to about 1930—the Albanian *Rilindja* (renaissance)—also saw the language standardised, and the first school to teach in Albanian opened.

In the twentieth century, Albania has produced a host of eminent writers; Ismail Kadare is perhaps the best-known internationally. Kadare, who was born in 1936, lives in Paris and is a prolific author. Many of his novels, poetry, and essays on Balkan politics have been translated. Although Kadare is seen as a controversial figure in Albania because of his close links with the former communist regime and their approval of his work, he is still respected as Albania's most important modern writer.

One of his best-known novels, *Prilli i thyer (Broken April)*, chronicles life in northern Albania's mountains and describes the influence of the Kanun, the body of traditional law codified by Lek Dukagjine. Despite the fact that Kadare comes from the south himself, many regard this novel as an authoritative work on northern culture and traditions. Albanian history is the subject of several of Kadare's novels: Gjergj Skenderbeg's fight against the Turks is treated in *Kështjella (The Castle)*, and the country's occupation by Italian forces during the Second World War is the backdrop to *Gjenerali i ushtris ësë vdekur (The General of the Dead Army)*.

History: from Skenderbeg to Hoxha

Although Albanians are descended from the Illyrians, an ancient tribe inhabiting the western Balkans, the first Albanian state was not recognised until the 12th century as the Arber Princedom. Various Albanian and Serbian princedoms competed for power over the next 200 years, but then the growing threat of Ottoman power culminated in the assimilation of Albania into the Ottoman empire after the battle of Kosova in 1389. In 1443, the Albanian prince Gjergj Kastrioti Skenderbeg led a rebellion against the Turks. This period (1443–68) was the first time that much of modern-day Albania was recognised as a unified state. Skenderbeg has since been celebrated as a national hero, and his image is to be found everywhere throughout Albania. The flag of Albania is the emblem of the Kastrioti family: a double-headed black eagle on a red background.

Nevertheless, with the death of Skenderbeg, Albania was to fall once more under Turkish rule and remain so until 1912 after the break-up of the Ottoman Empire in the Balkan wars of this period.

► *An image of Voskopjë before the Ottoman invasion.*

A NATIONAL HERO

The son of an Albanian lord, Gjergj Kastrioti grew up at the Ottoman court (a common practice to ensure his father's loyalty) and was trained in the Ottoman army. Renamed Iskander Bey—Skenderbeg—he fought in several campaigns and rose to high position; but in 1443 Skenderbeg turned against the Sultan. He captured his father's seat in Krujë and, as legend has it, raised the Kastrioti flag with the words: 'I have not brought you liberty, I found it here, among you'. In 1444 Skenderbeg united Albania's princes under the League of Lezhë. For the next 25 years, he used his diplomatic skills in securing Italian support for his military campaigns against the Ottoman army: its kings and popes were keen to champion a leader fighting a rising Muslim empire.

▲ Ardinicë monastery dates back to the 13th century and is now the seat of the Greek Orthodox church in Albania; the mosque in Gjirokastër used to be an Orthodox church before the Ottoman invasion.

On 28 November 1912 Albania's independence was declared at a summit held in Vlorë on the coast. Ismail Qemali, a leading nationalist intellectual, led the summit and created a temporary government. Albanian independence was discussed among the great powers of the time, Great Britain, France, Russia, Germany, Austria-Hungary, and Italy, at a Conference in London dealing with the dissolution of the Ottoman Empire. This resulted in the establishment of the borders of the Albanian state which have remained unchanged. The imposed borders excluded more than half of Albania's former lands which were inhabited by Albanians, such as Kosovo in modern day Yugoslavia and large parts of Western Macedonia. This is still a point of grievance among Albanians today, and can also be held to blame for much of the region's current tensions. The Conference also gave Albania an independent and neutral status under the protection of the Great Powers. The German prince Wilhelm zu Wied was assigned as the new country's sovereign. An International Control Committee drew up Albania's first Organisational Statute in 1914 and acted as a supervisory and regulatory body for Albanian government administration and finances.

▼ According to legend, Skenderbeg was married at Ardinicë monastery.

During the First World War Albania maintained its neutral status, and in 1920, Albania's first parliament was elected. This parliament approved the country's first two constitutions in 1920 and 1922. However, conflict between the two political parties—one of which represented the land-owning classes reluctant to give up their feudal power, and the other of which aimed to build a Western-style democracy—led to the revolution of 1924. A new democratic government was formed under the leadership of the Greek Orthodox bishop Fan Noli, but at the end of 1924, Noli's main opponent Ahmet Zogu, aided by the Serbs, seized power. In 1928 Zog declared himself the King of Albania and ruled as such until the Italian invasion of Albania in 1939.

The aftermath of the second world war

Mussolini saw Albania as a strategic bridge in his plans to invade Greece. However, Italian rule was chaotic, and after a disastrous campaign against the Greeks and the Allied invasion of Italy in 1943, German forces occupied Albania. After a bitter resistance struggle by Albanian partisans, Albania was liberated in November 1944. The Communist-led partisans under the leadership of Enver Hoxha immediately assumed power, with help from the Russian and Yugoslav governments. Hoxha then proceeded to put in place one of the most brutal dictatorships in Eastern Europe, built on a personality cult centred on himself and his Party of Labour. As a result of Hoxha's dogmatic adherence to Stalinism, Albania became increasingly isolated internationally. In 1948 Hoxha severed ties with Tito in Yugoslavia; in 1960 he broke with the Soviet Union, in opposition to Krushchev's attempts to erase Stalin's legacy from Soviet life. After 1960 the Albanian regime formed a close relationship with Mao Tse Tung's Communist China, but following Mao's death and subsequent reforms in China, Albania severed all ties with its only remaining ally in 1978. The years after 1978 saw an intensification of the personality cult around Hoxha and his paranoia about foreign intrigue and conspiracy. Albania became completely isolated from the rest of the world as he embarked upon a massive programme to safeguard Albania against foreign invasion. Hoxha's regime had more than 700,000 concrete bunkers constructed and amassed an arsenal of conventional weapons.

▼ A typical image from communist times: Enver Hoxha waves to the cheering crowds during a parade in Tiranë in 1981.

Once relations with China came to an end, all economic aid from abroad ceased. Hoxha's increasingly paranoid schemes and Albania's economic and political isolation brought the country closer and closer to the brink. By the late 1980s, Eastern Europe's most completely centralised planned economy was on the verge of economic collapse.

For the older generation in Albania, who have lived under a communist regime for most of their lives, the rapid and chaotic changes of the past ten years have been particularly confusing and difficult to take in. Many older people are beginning to express some nostalgia for the communist past; they are finding it hard to come terms with the disappearance of the society and all its reference points that they once knew. Even former political prisoners can be heard lamenting that the order that existed during communism has disappeared. Many of these people are now saying that perhaps communism wasn't such a bad thing after all, and that perhaps the problem was Enver Hoxha, not the system itself.

▲ *One of many bunkers that still litter Albania's countryside. Many farmers are now labouring to dig up these annoying hindrances.*

The price of dissent

Hoxha's paranoia about conspiracy extended to his own citizens; he would tolerate no dissent, and thousands of Albanians were executed, sent to labour camps (in which many of them would die) or sent to work in remote rural areas as internal exiles. The state secret police, SIGURIMI, pervaded society at all levels, coercing people to inform on neighbours, colleagues, and friends.

Bledar Shaplo was a doctor in Korçë, one of Albania's largest southern cities close to the border with Greece. He became the director of Korçë's hospital, but in 1977 was arrested, charged with military espionage, and sentenced to be shot.

'I believe I was imprisoned simply because the SIGURIMI knew that I hated the communist regime. I was arrested and accused of making secret liaisons with Greek military officers. They were just looking for an excuse. They said I went out at night and this was when I met these officers. This was complete nonsense; I did go out at night, but I was visiting some of my patients. Fortunately I knew the Interior Minister at the time. He visited Korçë, and people told him that I was in prison. He ordered the sentence to be changed, so I was simply charged with speaking out against the system as opposed to military espionage.'

Bledar stayed in prison for five years; in 1982 he was released and sent into internal exile. He had to work as a doctor in a remote village in Burrel District in central Albania. 'Things were very difficult for me in prison, as well as for my family. My son tried to escape to Greece in 1980 and he was arrested and also put in prison. My daughter had been very good at school, but after I was arrested she was sent to work as a forestry labourer for 12 years. She is married now and lives in the USA and has become a lawyer. Once I was sent to Burrel I was separated from my wife and children, who went to Ersekë in southern Albania.' In 1991, the government passed a law that allowed political prisoners in exile to return to their homes. Bledar was free to leave the village. 'We had lost our home in Korçë and there were no opportunities in Ersekë, so we came to Tiranë. We had nowhere to live, and the state gave us a room in a factory that had shut down. It was very difficult there, as there were five of us in the one

▲ *Bledar Shaplo outside the apartment block in Tiranë where he lives with his wife and son.*

room and twelve families to one toilet. After living in that miserable place for three years, the association of ex-political prisoners helped my family and me and got us this new apartment. This has been a blessing for us.'

Bledar's pension is practically worthless, so the family survive on what his daughter sends from the USA. But things are still difficult for his son, who shares the new apartment. He has finished his studies in economics, but for the past five years has been able to find very little work. Bledar is worried about what he sees happening in Albania: 'Life is difficult because the government is corrupt, and there are too many old communists still in it. Only when we get rid of these people will we have democracy here; now, we have a democracy only on paper. Some people are even beginning to think that the time of Hoxha wasn't so bad. Everybody had a job and there was security in Hoxha's time—but look at the price we had to pay for it. I don't think we should go back to the old system, but I am disillusioned and confused. This is not the society I went to prison for.'

'We should forgive and forget, but it will take a long time'

Rizhvan Dellolli was imprisoned by the Hoxha regime and then sent into internal exile in the village of Eskaj near Lushnjë, south of Tiranë. He had to work on an agricultural co-operative: 'There were many people in internal exile in this village. It was a very difficult life for us. As political prisoners we were treated much worse than everybody else, even though life on the co-operative was miserable for everyone.'

All crops were grown for export, and workers only received a tiny ration. 'I remember when my father was dying. He said that before he died he wanted to taste a watermelon once more, like when he was a boy before communism. But you had to have the Director's authorisation to take a watermelon from the warehouse, which was a very complicated process, particularly if you were a political prisoner. I managed to get authorisation to take one watermelon from the warehouse. However, it took so long to get all the paperwork done that by the time I got back to the house with my watermelon, my father had died. I felt very sad.'

As a political prisoner, Rizhvan had to have special permission to go anywhere, and was constantly being watched by the SIGURIMI. Prisoners were convenient scapegoats for co-operative leaders if work targets were not fulfilled or if new ideas did not work. 'We would be accused of trying to sabotage the work ethics of the people and we could get sent to prison for up to ten years.' People in the village would not speak out against unfair practices because they feared being sent to prison as well. 'If you complained about such things this was interpreted as political.'

Rizhvan has remained in Eskaj with the rest of his family and is the Mayor of Bubullimë Commune. 'There have been good changes here: at least my children can continue their education; they were not allowed to go to university because I was a political prisoner. We can talk freely again: before, we were sometimes even afraid to greet people, because we were seen as enemies of the state and people were afraid to be seen with us or talk to us.' But Rizhvan does not feel that any of the changes have compensated him and his family for their suffering: 'There are very few opportunities for my children here. My son is a qualified teacher but he cannot survive on a teacher's salary here, and instead has to work as a simple labourer in Italy to help support our family. It is a tragedy for our country that all the talented people are leaving.'

Rizhvan also questions the efficacy of electoral democracy: 'The politicians now do not think of the country: they think they will only stay in power for two or three years and therefore just want to profit as much as they can from their positions. How can we build a new country if our politicians have this kind of attitude? Even Europe has not really been very supportive of real change here.' But he is worried that Albania is not leaving its past behind: 'There are a lot of people who used to be senior in the Communist Party who are gaining power and influence again. These people are creating problems for our society to move forward: they are used to ordering people around and like power for power's sake. They don't want to consult with people. I know we should forgive and forget, but given my experiences, and those of a lot of other people like me, it is going to be very hard and take a long time.'

▼ *This communist slogan reads: 'We are strictly relying on our own efforts'.*

The painful transition to democracy

Enver Hoxha died in 1985. Given the desperate state of the economy, his successor Ramiz Alia introduced some cautious reforms in 1989. In July 1990, about 5,000 Albanians desperately trying to seek asylum from an increasingly harsh economic and social crisis occupied foreign embassies in Tiranë. In December, Tiranë witnessed widespread student rioting, and the first opposition party (the Democratic Party) was formed and legalised. Riots continued throughout the winter and early 1991, leading to the first multi-party elections in March 1991.

The 'new' Albania is a parliamentary democracy: the elected People's Assembly chooses the President for a five-year term, who then appoints a Prime Minister to head the Council of Ministers. For administrative purposes, the country has 36 districts, whose governing structure is based on proportional representation.

The 1991 elections were won by a coalition of the Communist and Socialist parties led by Fatos Nano, but the deepening economic crisis made it impossible for him to govern. A period of general anarchy and chaos followed as the state gradually collapsed. Further elections in March 1992 were won by the DP under the leadership of Sali Berisha, which was to stay in power until the cataclysmic events of 1997. At first, Berisha's government gradually managed to restore order to the country and secure much-

▼ *A political rally during the 1992 election campaign, a time of optimism for most Albanians.*

'I felt that we could all die that day, but it didn't matter because it would be for something so worthwhile. For the first time in 50 years people were learning what it meant to give your life for your country. Even though the Communists had rammed it down our throats for 50 years, that day we were ready to give our lives for change.'

Blerinda Idrizi, speaking of her participation in a student demonstration in Skenderbeg Square in February 1991.

needed foreign aid. However, by 1994 the government was regarded as becoming increasingly corrupt and authoritarian. A constitution drafted by the DP that would have given Berisha sweeping powers over all aspects of government was roundly rejected in a referendum which many Albanians considered the first real test of their new democracy. But this rejection did not deter the government from trying to consolidate its power. Using foreign assistance from Europe, and aggressively manipulating public opinion in the West and at home to portray himself and his government as the only hope for stability in a country surrounded by Balkan crises, Berisha's government was able increase its stranglehold on power. The DP unsurprisingly declared a unanimous victory in the 1996 election, which was characterised by widespread reports of voter intimidation and vote-rigging. The USA and several Western European governments refused to recognise the results of the elections and threatened to reduce levels of aid to Albania significantly.

Nevertheless the DP managed to retain power and became even more authoritarian. Protests in Tiranë after the elections were brutally put down by riot police. Foreign observers warned that there were human-rights abuses in Albania relating to the muzzling of the opposition, which was denied its rights to organise and gather, and restricted from participating in the political arena. Journalists were increasingly being targeted and harassed by the police, and many Albanians felt alarm at the growing influence of the Albanian Secret Police, as well as the government's total monopolisation of television and radio.

▼ Streets and buildings are still showing the scars of the 1997 riots and looting.

Economic crisis: the collapse of the pyramid savings schemes

When informal investment schemes, commonly known as 'pyramid schemes', sprang up in 1993, millions of Albanians invested all their savings in the hope for free-market profits. Despite continual warning signs and the evident need for some sort of regulation of the informal investment market, the government did nothing. Many Albanians believe that government officials had major stakes in the pyramid schemes and as a result were reluctant to curb the exorbitant profits being made by the biggest pyramid firms.

In early 1997, there was a spectacular collapse of the pyramid firms, and millions of Albanians lost their life savings. The World Bank and IMF estimate the value of Albanians' deposits lost in the pyramid savings schemes at $1.2 billion, the equivalent of half of Albania's GDP for 1996. Widespread protests followed,

▲ As a result of Albania's economic isolation, even food supply proved a challenge during the early 1990s.

and on 2 March 1997 the government declared a state of emergency and imposed a curfew throughout the country. This intolerance towards political and civil opposition, as well as the increased presence of the army in southern Albania, sparked off violent unrest. Despite a compromise reached among the main political parties, the level of anarchy became unmanageable, culminating in widespread looting of arms depots by the frustrated civilian population. A coalition government led by the Socialist President Rexhep Medani and Prime Minister Fatos Nano tried to govern the country after the government's collapse, but until the arrival of an international peace-keeping force (mainly comprising troops from Italy and Greece) in April 1998, total anarchy reigned. Even with the presence of the peace-keeping force, governing the country still proved highly problematic given the large number of weapons in civilian hands.

By the end of the summer of 1997, sufficient law and order had been restored for state institutions to function again. Nevertheless, security remained a major problem, with the police force and army fairly ineffective in guaranteeing law and order. During 1998 there was a gradual return to normality, and at long last the country's first post-communist constitution was approved. It is widely accepted as a solid base on which to build a genuine democratic society in Albania, and a far cry from the farcical, authoritarian version drafted by the Berisha government in 1994. However, in September 1998 the murder of a leading opposition politician sparked armed rioting in Tiranë and the resignation of Prime Minister Fatos Nano. Nano's replacement, Pandeli Majko, was seen as having no past political associations, and people seemed to appreciate his youth and energy.

Judging on the basis of events since late 1999, Albania's political future seems to be at risk again. Fatos Nano has regained the leadership of the SP, ousting its youthful leader Pandeli Majko and replacing him as Prime Minister. At the same time, Sali Berisha, former President and leader of the DP, has returned from disgrace and is back at the helm of the DP. With elections likely in late 2000, the scene looks set for a resumption of the power struggle between Nano and Berisha, replacing serious political debates about the country's economic future and the multitude of pressing social problems. Western governments have voiced their concern over the return to prominence of both Berisha and Nano, and the USA has made it clear that it does not wish to see them contest in Albania's next election. It remains to be seen what influence outside governments and donors will have; either way, it will be the Albanian people who once more suffer as much-needed economic and social reform, and the outside funding required to support it, is hijacked by politicians' irresponsible power struggles.

One of the most urgent tasks for Albania's government is to persuade the civilian population to give up the weapons they have held since the riots of 1997. Efforts have proceeded at a snail's pace, and general banditry in the north is once more on the rise. Indeed, if the two main political opponents decided to rally supporters with words of aggression, this could have disturbing consequences. Both main parties are nurturing a political climate that is not far from the northern Albanian vendetta tradition, and, given the continuing influence of mafia elements within Albanian society and a climate of violence in neighbouring Kosovo, the region once more seems to be entering a period of insecurity and uncertainty.

Building a democracy

One of the biggest problems Albania faces in its political transformation is Albanians' lack of familiarity with the process of democracy and its accompanying dialogue, debate, and compromise. Albanians have not had the concept of democracy, and of individual and collective responsibilities, made clear to them, nor do they have any examples of to learn from in their own history. They see the state's function merely as controlling the excesses of individuals and society in general. This attitude absolves many Albanians of responsibility for their actions, as well as allowing for authoritarian excesses such as those of the Berisha government. The current political system does not provide Albanians with a model of democracy either: gaining power depends simply on how effectively one can prove that one is anti-communist. The media reflect this simplistic struggle for political power (and much of the press, radio, and television is still state-owned), which makes it difficult for people to make informed and unbiased choices. Albanians see their vote simply as a means to support whoever they feel is most violently opposed to communism and the past. There is very little discussion of how the parties propose to resolve Albania's economic and social problems; instead, the debate revolves around their political vendettas.

▼ Albanians are realising that democracy means more than just voting..

The relative irresponsibility of most politicians in Albania, and their ability to manipulate people's ignorance of democratic principles, have not created an environment for a genuine civil society. This has also ensured that the government is not held to account for its actions or failures to act. For instance, the Berisha government would justify its inefficiency and corruption by accusing the opposition of being sympathetic to communism and blocking reform. Such scare tactics have made Albania's social and political development painfully slow, as well as reinforcing old mentalities based on confrontation rather than dialogue and co-operation.

With the recent resignation of Pandeli Majko and return to power of Fatos Nano, coupled with increasing uncertainty over the future of Prime Minister Medani, Albania seems to be once more returning to the violent and wasteful political bickering that dominated the Berisha years. As a result, most Albanians initial optimism that they would finally get the democracy they longed for seems to be fading fast.

A chance to start anew: Blerinda and Arben's story

Blerinda studied at the University of Tiranë from 1986 to 1990, staying on to work as an assistant professor. Arben also graduated in 1990 but was sent to teach in a remote part of Mirditë District. Both of them witnessed the change in Albania's political climate and participated in the student riots from December 1990 to March 1991, which ultimately led to the fall of the Communist government. Blerinda describes her experience: 'During my last year of studies, things were starting to change a bit. We used to question why we weren't allowed to read banned books like Kafka. Because we were able to ask such questions—which my parents could never have done—we began to feel that things were going to change.

'In June 1990 the first people started to jump the fences of the foreign embassies to seek political asylum. On 2 July, thousands of people tried to get into the embassies in Tiranë. It was very dramatic, and we were sure that these people were going to be severely punished. To our surprise, nobody was killed or sent to prison. Instead, they were allowed to leave the country. I remember that date very well as Arben and I got engaged that day. Everyone was trying to escape, it was crazy. My father said to me, "Why are you and Arben getting engaged today? Just go and jump an embassy fence together and leave, this may be your only chance." But we decided not to. I'm not sure why, but I think we felt that leaving wasn't the right thing to do. However, at the end of our engagement ceremony I felt very sad because I heard that a lot of my closest friends had left. I felt very alone.'

▲ Arben and Blerinda in Skenderbeg Square, where in 1990 they joined others to protest against the Communist regime.

In December 1990 the student riots began, and the Democratic Party was legalised, so people felt that real change was possible at last. Blerinda was skeptical: 'I still didn't believe that things would change that fast, or for the better. I felt this because people were approaching the changes in the old way—with so much hatred. People wanted revenge. Some of us argued that we should forgive and forget, but we were shouted down, and people accused us of being sympathetic to the past. It was very difficult to be reasonable; you often felt that you were swimming against the tide.'

Teaching at school in Kaçinar in late 1990, Arben and his friends used to listen to the Voice of America on the radio to hear about the events in Tiranë, although they knew that they could be arrested for doing so. 'When we heard of the student demonstrations in Tiranë, we were really thrilled. I rushed down to Tiranë to stay for a week and join the demonstrations.' He lost his job as a result: 'I was very happy about this though, because I was able to go back to Tiranë and join in all the demonstrations. Blerinda and I were very happy to be part of the demonstration that brought down the statue of Enver Hoxha in the main square in Tiranë in February 1991.' Blerinda and Arben will never forget this exciting time: 'We felt we wanted to make a contribution and support the changes. We were excited to find so many other people who believed in change and a new future.'

A time of disillusionment

In spite of their initial optimism, Blerinda and Arben decided to try to emigrate to the USA in April 1991. Most of their friends had left, and they were alarmed at how things were changing: 'so much of it seemed to be based on revenge and hatred.' Because of visa problems, Blerinda and Arben ended up staying in Bucharest, Romania, for a year and a half. Blerinda found work, but 'in December 1992 we decided to return to Albania. It was difficult to make this decision, because in Albania, once you have left people tend to see you as a failure if you come back. We travelled back to Tiranë by bus, and it was very emotional for me. We got to see how everything was breaking down or had been destroyed. I was very sad. Everything was broken and dirty, and there were bars on all the shop windows. It was not a country that I recognised anymore. Everything and everyone was miserable, and nobody seemed to have any hope. I saw my country helpless and hopeless.'

Blerinda and Arben found it very hard to find jobs, despite their education. The situation improved in 1993, according to Belinda: 'There was a good group of people in the new government who were trying to change things for the better. People saw this and were supportive. The best people in the country were being listened to, and this instilled hope in people. I think 1993 was the only year in which the Albanian people were genuinely listened to.'

Arben, who found work in the Ministry of Justice, describes what happened as the Berisha government settled into power: 'In my job I got to see how the new government was working, but I soon became very disillusioned. Gradually, especially as they worked on the new constitution, they became more authoritarian and concerned with hanging on to power. They wanted to make their political interests the law, just like in the old days. I couldn't accept this and decided to leave my job.'

Blerinda was shocked to find that history was repeating itself: 'At this time, if you had courage to speak up the government had ways of silencing you. I couldn't believe this was happening again. My parents had been two of the original 300 supporters of the DP. In 1994 things started to get bad with the DP, and my parents, my mother in particular, felt they had to speak up. Twenty years earlier, when they were university professors, Hoxha had run a campaign to "democratise" social studies. Hoxha encouraged academics to speak up and be critical of the regime—but this was simply a front so he could find out who was against him. As a result, many people were put in jail; my parents were sent into internal exile. Now, 20 years later, as my mother spoke up I saw the same kind of intimidation against her. I was shocked and deeply saddened. Things got more difficult, and my mother had to leave the country and went to the United States. My father joined her the following year.'

Arben comments on Albanians' lack of democratic experience which brought Berisha back to power in spite of his government's inefficiency: 'People were misled by a very bad election campaign. Berisha frightened people by saying, "If you don't vote for me, the communists will come back to power for sure". People were so afraid of this that they would do anything to prevent it. People were also manipulated because 70 per cent of our population is still rural and does not have the benefit of a good education.' Blerinda, who is now working with an American humanitarian agency, adds: 'I feel sad for what is happening here. There are so many good people here, but they are not allowed to have their voice. They must be supported, and people must stop placing blind faith in the government solving all our problems. We must start to take responsibility. But this is still a new concept for people here, and it will take time.'

▼ *Water cannons being fired against protesters in Skenderbeg Square, 1991.*

The legacy of central planning

Albania had the most rigid centrally planned economy of any country in Eastern Europe, based on a strict adherence to Stalinist principles. Massive industrial complexes were built throughout the country, with the intention of transforming Albania's predominantly rural peasant society into an urban industrial one practically overnight. But despite such grandiose plans, reality proved to be far different. By 1992 most of the factories lay in ruins or idle, and Albania's population was still 70 per cent rural with thousands of people unemployed. Albania's isolation from the rest of the world following its break with China in 1978 meant that its factories (which were already using outdated Chinese technology) rapidly became obsolete. This, coupled with a greatly diminished market for its exports and serious inefficiencies in the system of agricultural collectives, had brought Albania to a state of complete economic collapse by 1991.

Albania's first democratically elected government was faced with the daunting task of reversing 50 years of economic mismanagement and inefficiency, in order to satisfy an electorate suffering extreme hardship. Despite the Berisha government's serious weaknesses, it was still faced with an almost impossible task. Under pressure from international financial institutions, it undertook a draconian structural adjustment programme. Official statistics showed Albania having the highest economic growth rate in all the post-communist countries of Eastern Europe, but the reform programme brought even greater hardship to Albanians. Much of the growth was financed by remittances from Albanians working abroad and manifested itself in artificially high levels of

▼ *The ferro-nickel mines at Prenjas used to employ 2,000 workers but closed in 1991.*

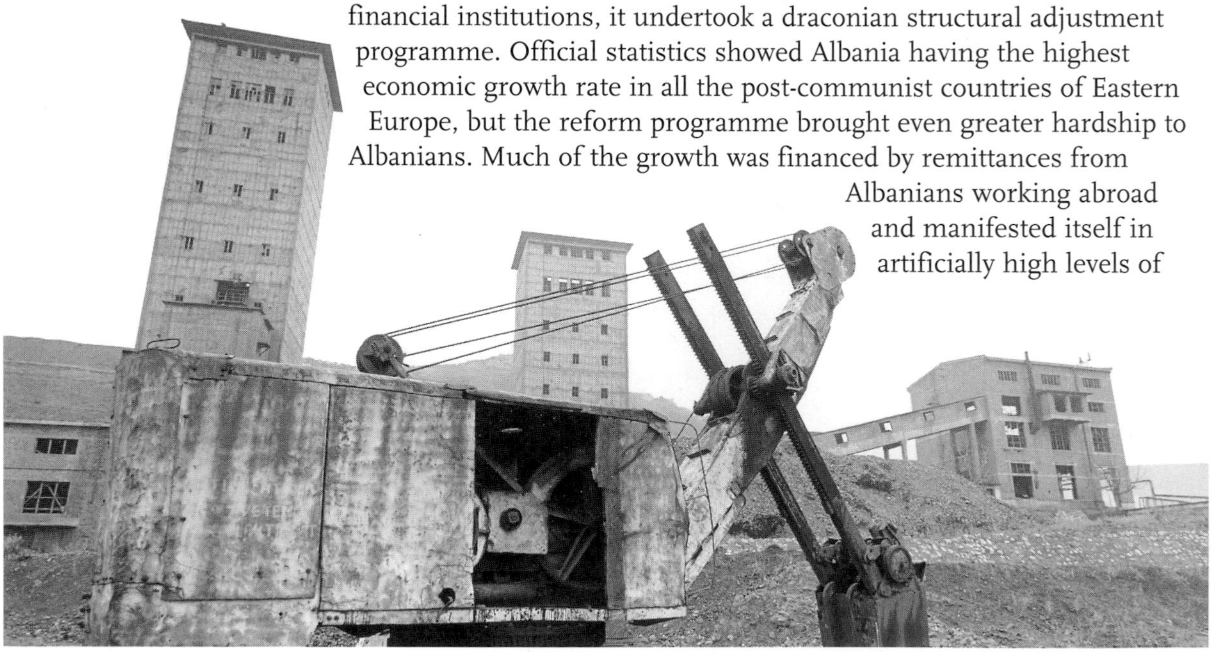

consumption of imported goods. At the same time, infrastructure continued to deteriorate. Albania's meagre road network continued to fall apart, making main sections of national roads almost impassable at times; water became a scarce commodity in cities, particularly during the summer; and power cuts in the winter lasted anywhere from a few hours to a few weeks. During the summer, water was rationed to a few hours a day and in winter, electricity was rationed to the same degree.

As a result of the anarchy and chaos of 1991–92, approximately 60–70 per cent of Albania's population suddenly found themselves unemployed. Because a great number of Albanians started migrating to Italy and Greece in search of work from 1992, unemployment halved during 1993. In the period up to 1997 the number of people registered as unemployed has remained high at about 15–20 per cent, although most people estimate that the real figure was at least 10–20 per cent higher. It is a persistent phenomenon that an estimated 40 per cent of Albania's labour force, 400,000 people, are working outside Albania at any given time.

Former employees of the Elbasan steelworks have taken on the challenge of privatisation.

A past triumph: the steelworks in Elbasan

The city of Elbasan was home to one of the largest steelworks in Eastern Europe. Built with assistance from the Chinese, the massive complex dominates the landscape around Elbasan. Hoxha viewed it as one of the great triumphs of the Albanian revolution. The reality however, was slightly different: giant smokestacks belched appalling amounts of industrial pollution across a wide area, and workers laboured under inhuman conditions with little or no regard to their health. With communism's collapse in 1991–92, the factory all but shut down. A few smelters still work today and, with even less regulation than under communism, continue to cast a pall of dirty smog over Elbasan. Of the thousands of workers who were employed at the steelworks when it was fully functional, some, like Xheyahir Boriei and a few of his fellow workers, have been able to benefit from the privatisation of some of the steelworks' smaller workshops. 'I worked here as an engineer from 1965 to 1992, when the factory stopped working and I lost my job. In 1994 some parts of the factory became available for rent. My friends and I got together and managed to get the use of this workshop and the machinery that was left in it. A lot of it had been damaged, destroyed, or even stolen. Although we rent the workshop from the government, we have managed to buy most of the equipment. We make gas for bottled drinks and other uses.'

During the anarchy of 1997, Xheyahir and his partners lost a lot of money and had equipment stolen. But he feels confident that things will start to get better. 'We just want to work, we don't care about politics. I think since 1997 people have finally understood that we cannot go on like we were before and that we have to think about the future, not just today. Even though the continuing violence is terrible, sometimes we joke that maybe all the criminals will eventually eliminate each other. I always believed that one day we would have the freedoms we have now. I work independently now and for myself, whereas before we had to depend on others and had no control. Life in this factory was terrible under communism. It caused a lot of sickness, and the government did nothing.'

Xheyahir intends to keep working in spite of remaining doubts about security. However, his daughter does not share his confidence and has decided to emigrate to Canada. 'I am sad she is leaving, because it is a shame that we are losing all our bright young people, and this will make it difficult for our country to move forward.'

But many Albanians are still not familiar with private business, as Xheyahir explains: 'Our business is growing and we managed to keep all the clients we had got by 1997. Although it is not easy, we make enough money to have a reasonable life. We will build slowly, but we hope the government will be supportive of us. We would like to expand but it is very difficult to get a loan; the banks don't trust us and still have the old communist mentality that we are here for them and not the other way around. In Albania, because of communism we still have a mentality among some people that we should not have to work hard and that the state will take care of all our problems. This is what happened to the people who lost everything in the pyramid schemes: they wanted to get rich quickly without having to work for it. Some people are jealous of our success, and sometimes threaten us. If we were afraid of this, we would just give up. But becoming too afraid to work would be the worst thing. If we don't give up then there is hope. Fortunately, there are a lot of people who think like us.'

Agriculture: after the collectives

One sector of the economy which has been relatively successful is small-scale farming, especially in the coastal plains' Mediterranean climate and fertile soils. Despite a traumatic break-up of the communist collectives and some land ownership disputes, land redistribution has proceeded relatively smoothly. Each family that used to belong to a collective received $4,700m^2$ of land. Greenhouses have become very popular and profitable; Lakeh Kaya and his brother, who farm in the village of Eskaj near Lushnjë, have had theirs for two years now. 'We had a good year last year with the greenhouse and worked hard. Our

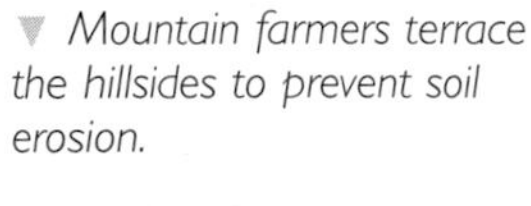

▼ *Mountain farmers terrace the hillsides to prevent soil erosion.*

results were so good that we were able to get another 1,000m² under production. Even though we can't get credit from the bank, we managed to borrow some money from family and friends, and this has helped us to put up the second greenhouse.' Because of high transport costs, farmers can find it difficult to get their produce to market: 'Most of it goes to Tiranë and Vlorë. Someone in the village has a van, and we pay him for transport. Vlorë and Lushnjë are closer, but Tiranë is a bigger market, and the prices are better. There is a lot of competition, but we still manage to make a profit and save some money each year.'

▲ *Lakeh Kaya in his greenhouse. His entire family helps with planting.*

Like the steelworkers in Elbasan, Lakeh has not had much external support for his business: 'The land here used to produce a lot of corn and wheat, but now this is too expensive, and there are no banks to give us credit. Also, the government imports too much wheat and we cannot compete. The government doesn't really support us, and the local government has no power to do anything.'

The Kaya brothers are not yet working with other farmers in order to bring down costs, because they are afraid of being cheated or exploited. 'We are a little bit suspicious about working with other people after 50 years of communism. I think we are still allergic to co-operatives. But I know that I cannot grow stronger alone; we will get together with people who are hard workers. For too long under communism we supported lazy people who didn't want to work. I have worked hard and invested a lot, and I am not prepared to risk this with someone who is not serious.'

Not many people have left Eskaj, so there is not much extra land for sale. Lakeh wonders what will happen when he has to divide up his land among his sons: 'If everybody else does the same, then our land will get smaller and smaller. But while the older people here are reluctant to go to the city, the younger people are attracted to Tiranë. My son says that he would rather be in the city than have to wear my old gumboots all day. If he can go to the city and find a good job, then I don't mind; it will relieve some of the pressure on the land.'

In order to improve rural life in Albania, Lakeh is convinced that local government must have more authority. 'They are more interested in our problems than the politicians in Tiranë. I am worried that we don't have a health clinic here—the government should help us with this. If I had enough money, I would build one for the village, as would other successful farmers. If our country is to move forward, we must have good services in rural areas. I want to do something for my country and the people here. If we all think this way then we can really develop our country.'

Water Carrier

In villages far from natural springs or wells, women have traditionally carried water over far distances in special containers. NGOs are working with villagers to improve water supply in remote areas.

Rural poverty

Apart from shops filled with foreign goods and hundreds of dilapidated Mercedes Benz in the streets (many of them brought in illegally from Western Europe), it is hard to find any tangible evidence of the 'Albanian economic miracle'. What little development had taken place since the end of communism was almost wiped out during the chaos of 1997 and Albania has had to start again in rebuilding its shattered economy. While there is a general consensus that people are marginally better off than they were under communism, making ends meet is still a major challenge for most Albanian families. There was a serious lack of investment during the 1990s in the development of rural communities in Albania, particularly in the north of the country. Although the government managed to ensure that people in rural areas received a basic welfare allowance that covered their immediate subsistence needs, there was practically no investment in social or physical infrastructure.

Due to their proximity to Greece, people in rural southern Albanian communities were able to mitigate the harshness of the economic situation by migrating to gain seasonal employment there. Most of the villages of the south are still devoid of young people for much of the year, due to the availability of employment in the Greek construction, agriculture, and tourist sectors. In the north, however, such opportunities were not so readily available. During the war in Bosnia, many people in northern towns such as Shkodër survived by breaking the UN embargo with Yugoslavia, trading in fuel and other essential commodities. With the 1996 Dayton peace accords, this lucrative business suddenly and rapidly

► *Small-scale farmers add to their income by selling their produce at the roadside.*

came to an end. Thousands of people in remote and isolated mountain villages, often several hours' walk from the nearest road, were left to eke out a meagre subsistence on the tiny plots of land they had been allocated after the break-up of the collective system. Education and health facilities in such areas became almost non-existent. Despite the warnings of local people and international non-government organisations (NGOs), the government and international donors continued to ignore the plight of people in the north, dismissing these areas as economically unsustainable.

▼ *Makeshift houses in Kamza, built without permission or infrastructure by people who come in search of a better life in Tiranë.*

The consequence of the government's and donors' short-sightedness was a migration unprecedented in scale of villagers from the north to Tiranë and other major towns, especially Shkodër. With little money and no property rights, thousands of people from Albania's rural north settled on the outskirts of Tiranë in a desperate search for a better life. Huge shantytowns like Kamza have expanded without public infrastructure such as water, electricity, and sewerage. The public health hazards that are coming to light in places like Kamza are enormous, and cases of cholera and dysentery have already been witnessed. The new government and international donors have taken steps to address the needs of such communities as well as to channel direct assistance more effectively to the north. However, much still needs to be done to stem the flow of thousands of northerners to the shantytowns around Durrës and Tiranë. The sense of frustration and hopelessness, as well as growing poverty in places like Kamza, was one of the key sparks that ignited the violence of 1997.

► *A symbol of affluence, parked outside local government buildings in Korçë.*

The increase in unemployment and lack of economic and social investment during the 1990s coincided with the growth of pyramid investment schemes. These schemes lured millions of Albanians to invest the remittances that family members sent from abroad, in return for unrealistic interest rates which in some cases promised up to 50 per cent a month. The interest earned from pyramid schemes enabled thousands of Albanians who had no employment or other form of income to survive the period from 1992-97 despite the parlous state of the economy. The

▲ *Broz Marku, a successful farmer, did not fall prey to the get-rich-quick schemes, but chose to invest in his farm.*

complete collapse of these schemes in 1997, and Albanians' lack of experience with free markets and financial planning, eradicated the life savings of thousands of Albanians overnight. It also served to ignite the social conflict that had been brewing since 1992 and resulted in the destruction and looting of what little productive capacity Albania had managed to restore. In December 1997 200,000 people were officially registered as unemployed, and it is estimated that the same number of people out of work were simply not registering. According to the UNDP, unemployment was increasing at the alarming rate of 4,000 to 5,000 people per month in 1998.

Despite such gloomy statistics, Albanians are trying hard to rebuild their lives after the events of 1997. Broz Marku is a successful local farmer in the village of Gajnollë near Shkodër. Despite many challenges, he and his wife did not fall prey to the pyramid schemes and instead worked hard to build up their farm. They have gained a great deal of respect in their community as a result of their success and have given some of their land to an NGO project which is providing support to local farmers. As Broz says: 'My wife and I decided to invest our profits from the farm back into the farm and not into the pyramid schemes. Other people thought we were crazy and said, "Why do you work so hard when, if you join the pyramid schemes, you will get rich quickly without having to work?" However, when their pyramids collapsed, our investment stayed intact. I often say to people that they shouldn't base their dreams on something they cannot see and touch. I think many people have realised this even though they found the events of 1997 very painful.'

While the continuing lack of law and order add to the challenges, there is hope that the 1998 constitution will be able to provide a more lasting framework for such initiatives and enable the state to provide greater support for economic development. Furthermore, as people like Broz, the Kaya brothers, and Xheyahir continue to gain respect in their communities, others may follow their examples, and excesses like the pyramid schemes may be avoided in the future.

► *A tangible investment.*

In search of a living: the lure of Europe

Before 1991, the ability to travel outside of Albania was restricted to a select minority who the communist regime considered politically sound. For the vast majority of Albanians, the outside world was a complete unknown; the warped propaganda fed to them by Hoxha's regime extolled the virtues of Albania's socialist paradise, and compared it to the misery and wretchedness of everyday life for workers in capitalist countries. But thousands of Albanians would watch Italian and Greek broadcasts which the communist regime, despite their best efforts, failed to block. The images of the rest of Europe that Albanians saw on Italian and Greek television programmes contrasted dramatically with what the government told them. Albanians were desperate to have links with the rest of the world and to have the opportunity to travel.

As Albania's once phenomenal border security system started to crack in 1990, it opened the door for a floodgate of refugees seeking a better life in Western Europe. As the country's economic crisis deepened in 1991, thousands of Albanians fled to Italy and Greece in search of work. This was to become a permanent facet of Albanian life: since 1992, emigration has become the single most important means Albanian families use to survive. It is hard to find an Albanian family which does not have at least one family member working in Greece or Italy.

▼ Waiting outside the Greek Consulate in Gjirokastër.

▲ Travel agencies have opened all over Albania.

For many Albanian emigrants, life is not easy. Often the only option is to cross the border illegally, particularly to Greece, and Albanians consequently live under the constant fear of deportation. Much of the work they are able to get is seasonal, low paid, and in very menial occupations: it is not uncommon, especially among younger people, to find trained teachers or doctors working as waiters in Italy or as agricultural and construction workers in Greece. However, they will be earning five or six times what they would earn in Albania (a teacher's salary is about $60 a month).

According to research by the United Nations Development Programme, an estimated 40 per cent of Albania's population aged 19 to 40 have emigrated. At conservative estimates, in 1998 Greece was home to up to 400,000 Albanian immigrants, and Italy to 100–150,000. Using the same data, it is estimated that in the case of Greece, there is one Albanian for every 25–30 Greeks.

Of the 100,000 Albanian immigrants working in Italy in 1997 only 62,000 were there legally, while in Greece only 10,000 of the 350,000 immigrants were legal; the rest had crossed the Greek border on foot through the mountains—an option which is also dangerous because of the presence of the Albanian mafia. Because young men are seen as traditional breadwinners, they make up between two-thirds and three-quarters of Albanian immigrants in these countries.

Emigration is now seen as a normal way of earning money, so young men are often expected to spend time in Greece or Italy each year to support the rest of the family. As a result, at least 15 per cent of Albania's population are outside the country throughout the year. Although the Albanian government has signed seasonal employment agreements with Greece and Italy, the thousands of Albanians in search of employment who are unable to get the necessary paperwork will continue to go illegally if they are left with no other option.

Coping with negative stereotypes

Albanian emigrants have not found it easy to integrate in society in their host countries. The foreign media have consistently painted a highly negative picture of Albania and Albanians in general, dwelling on images of wild, gun-toting teenagers and the chaos of 1997. Albania is depicted as a lawless country populated by ruthless criminals. This stereotype has not helped Albanians abroad: emigrants speak of open discrimination, and in Italy, there have been cases of intimidation. The Italian media, particularly in the country's more right-wing northern region, blame illegal Albanian immigrants for much of the organised crime in the area. While the presence of the Albanian mafia in Italy is an issue for concern, it is not on the scale portrayed.

In Greece, negative stereotypes of Albanian immigrants have arisen because people do not understand conditions in Albania, and because of nationalist sentiments regarding the Greek minority in Albania. However, on an individual level, many Albanian emigrants speak kindly of their Greek employers and hosts. In Italy, several national NGOs are working with Albanian communities to secure better rights and working conditions for them, and there is a wealth of Italian NGOs working in Albania. Nevertheless, alienation and discrimination are likely to remain an unfortunate aspect of life for Albanians working in Greece and Italy, especially given the large numbers of illegal immigrants in these countries. Yet frustration about the rate of progress and economic necessity will continue to drive thousands of Albanians abroad in search of a better life.

▼ *Mountain routes are not always safe to travel.*

'This isn't much of a life for us': Kastriot's story

Kastriot from Pogradec has been working seasonally in Greece since 1991. His modest two-room house overlooks the wrecks of several Albanian Railways locomotives destroyed during the looting and rioting of 1997: 'People came from Korçë and Pogradec to take the aluminium from these locomotives to sell for scrap. I was working in Greece at the time, but I was shocked to see the damage when I came back.'

▲ *The remnants of the railway station at Pogradec, damaged during 1997. Trains are now running again.*

When Kastriot is in Albania, he helps his family and looks after their animals. He feels that apart from this there is nothing for him to do, so for eight months of the year he travels to Greece to work as an agricultural labourer. 'It is difficult to work in Greece, and the work is hard. People treat me well sometimes, and at other times not so well. It depends on what kind of relationship I have with my employer. Some of them feel sorry for us, others think we are bad people because of what they hear and see in the papers and on radio and television.'

As a farm worker in Greece, Kastriot receives board and lodging and usually earns between 3,500 and 5,000 drachma (about $15–$20) in a day. 'It would take me almost two weeks to make that kind of money here—if I could find a job. When we work in the tobacco fields, we start at three in the morning and work for up to twelve hours. Sometimes we fall asleep in the field. From what I hear, the Greeks treat us better than the Italians, so I would rather go to Greece than Italy. If I could earn 7,000 drachma ($30) a day then I would be very satisfied.'

Kastriot has worked for his current employer, who helps him get a work permit, for four years. He finds travel difficult on both sides of the border: 'The Greek authorities make things very difficult for us, although Greek people themselves are no problem for the most part. Our Albanian police give me a problem about anything that I try to bring back, and if I go illegally across the mountains, there are mafia waiting for us to steal our wages. I am angry with the police; they just make my life difficult, but at the same time they do nothing to catch the mafia who rob us in the mountains.'

Even with work permits, Albanian migrant workers have few rights if there is a dispute with an employer. 'A few years ago, when I worked for a different farmer, the Albanian workers in our area complained about working conditions and asked for a wage increase. The Greek farmers called the police, and we got thrown out of our rooms and sent into the mountains; but they did not have us deported. After three days, they called us back. Our conditions were unchanged—they just wanted to show us who was boss. Because a lot of us are working there illegally, we have to be careful what we do, and we have no rights. Things are getting better now, and the authorities are making it easier to get a work permit; I hope this will give us better conditions and rights when we are working there.'

Kastriot and his wife want to start a family, but the need to have a secure job, and fears over crime in Albania, have influenced their plans: 'I miss my wife when I am away, and this isn't much of a life for us. If I had the chance to go to Greece permanently and take my family with me, I would go, but I don't think I would go forever. I worry about my family's security here. My wife and I want to have only one child, and we hope it is a boy, because the mafia might try to kidnap a girl when she is older and send her to Italy. I would be happier here in Albania if I had enough money for my wife and the child we want to have, and if the state could guarantee their security. I hope that things will get better one day and I can either leave here altogether, or the economy will improve so that I can find a good job here.'

'One day I would like to come back': Albania's younger generation

The desire to leave Albania permanently is particularly strong among younger people. Many of them feel betrayed by the lack of political, economic, and social progress since the start of student protests against the communist regime. A lot of young people argue that they have little to show for their struggles for democracy in 1990–91, and that their idealism and aspirations for the future have been hijacked by a generation of older politicians who are still entrenched in the past. The tragic and violent events of 1997 proved a watershed for Albania's younger generation: until then, they felt that they had a chance to influence and shape Albania's future. For many young people, 1997 shattered these aspirations, and left most of them feeling that their future lay outside Albania.

Bledi Shllakut and Iannis Mitros are students in their final year at the University of Gjirokastër. Bledi comes from Tiranë, and Iannis is an Albanian ethnic Greek from Sarandë on the

Iannis Mitros and Bledi Shllakut in the hills around Gjirokastër, discussing the prospects of younger people in Albania.

coast. Although they would both like to stay in Albania, they are concerned about the lack of opportunities, according to Bledi. 'When we graduate I think it is better to try to emigrate, given the state of things here. Most of us think this way: if we have the opportunity we'll go. It is better to go abroad than stay here and work as a teacher for $65 a month.' But at the same time, Bledi is very aware that his generation will bear the main burden of rebuilding Albania: 'Our parents have left us nothing, and we have to start from nothing. We are young and we have to build something to give to our children. It is not like in my parents' generation, when the state took care of you. Now there is no state.'

Having lived through Eastern Europe's turbulent recent history, Bledi is critical of Albania's post-communist leaders: 'Maybe one day I'll come back, but there must be security and equal opportunities for all. In other East European countries, they started democracy properly. They told people that they have to work and gave them the laws and opportunities to do this. Here, it was a pseudo-democracy. The politicians didn't tell people that they had to work in order to build something for themselves. Work will build Albania, not things like smuggling and pyramid schemes. The politicians' behaviour demonstrated that it is okay to make money through illegal activities.'

▼ *The streets of Gjirokastër, where Iannis and Bledi study.*

Disillusioned by the lack of engagement with his generation's ideas and demands, Bledi finds it hard to imagine a better future. 'It is difficult for us as students. We try to challenge old mentalities, but people just say "go away, student"—especially in Gjirokaster, which is a lot more conservative than Tiranë. You can only be told to "go away" so many times until you decide to go away for good. You still feel that you would like to come back if things improve, but if you wait too much, you grow old. Albania has always been in crisis throughout its history. There is always a sense of insecurity here. Maybe it is our nature: maybe we are impatient and thus never resolve anything.'

Iannis shares Bledi's sense of frustration. Although he can easily find work in Greece because of his ethnic Greek status, he is unsure where his future lies. 'We want to go somewhere where we can realise our ambitions and dreams. All of us would like to stay here and create something, but there is no opportunity here.' Still, being able to emigrate does not solve Iannis's problems as an Albanian: 'A lot of people say to me, "It's easy for you to go to Greece, so why don't you just go?" But it is still not easy for me. When I am in Greece I feel more Albanian than Greek, and when I am in Albania I feel more Greek than Albanian—maybe I just need to go somewhere completely new. But home is here, and one day I would like to come back.'

Education: changing needs and ideas

Albania's political and economic transition has had a severe impact on the country's education system. Despite a strict and ideologically motivated educational system that was based on learning by rote, rather than open discussion and teaching students to think for themselves, Albania managed to achieve one of the highest literacy rates in Europe through universal primary education. Retired teacher Dhori Llora from Voskopojë explains the dilemmas faced by teachers during the Hoxha regime: 'As a teacher under communism, we were not there to watch and nurture children's individual intelligence and development. We were not there to support their understanding of the world according to their personal experience; instead, we had to turn them into robots. As a teacher, I found this very demoralising as we were stunting the cultural and intellectual development of our youth. This is not why people want to teach. Our schools were like factories, producing the product the Party wanted, rather than true places of learning.'

▲ Dhori Llora, who was a teacher under communism.

On account of its highly ideological basis, the education system represented one of the most significant symbols of communist oppression, and schools throughout Albania were destroyed during the chaos of 1991–92. While it is understandable that people wanted to vent their frustration, the destruction of educational facilities has been a major impediment to revitalising the education sector.

The state of schools in Albania's rural areas is particularly alarming: many primary school children study in classrooms with few desks and chairs or blackboards. Often, windows are missing, and without any sort of heating, children are hard pressed to concentrate on their studies during winter, which in the mountains can be extremely severe. Furthermore, it is increasingly difficult to find qualified teachers willing to work in rural areas, particularly the more isolated parts of Albania's north. Given the poor state of village schools and the scarcity of teachers, especially at the secondary

▼ A classroom that boasts basic heating.

school level, it is increasingly common to find families not bothering to send their children to school at all. Secondary school enrolment in rural areas has seen a persistent decline since 1992. This is a worrying trend as statistics show that a large number of young male secondary school drop-outs end up involved in some form of criminal activity. Recent studies by the United Nations Development Programme and local NGOs show that half of all crimes carried out during the anarchy of 1997 were committed by minors and young people under 26 years, with the majority of these being young men who had not finished school.

The breakdown in the educational system is partly caused by a lack of trained teachers. An average teacher's salary in Albania is 10,000 Lek per month ($80). As a result, many qualified teachers have given up teaching for better paid jobs in the private sector, or have chosen to leave the country. The UNDP notes that during 1996 and 1997, of 372 newly qualified grade school teachers only 195 accepted the positions they were offered. For junior secondary schools the results are similar: of the 1,900 newly qualified teachers less than half accepted the jobs on offer.

The consequence of such statistics is that more and more teachers are allowed to work in schools without the proper qualifications. Sotiraq Grozi, head teacher of the primary school in the village of Voskopojë near Korçë in southern Albania, has to manage this situation. 'Two of our teachers here come from Korçë every day. It is getting harder and harder to find teachers willing to teach in village schools like this one. Out of the 37 teachers in this Commune, only 20 actually have a teaching qualification. Qualified teachers, like many of the families here, are going to Greece where they get better pay and working conditions, and some are even going to America, Canada and Germany.'

The first school to teach in Albanian in Elbasan, now a museum.

Albania has one national university in Tiranë, and five regional universities in Shkodër, Elbasan, Vlorë, Korçë, and Gjirokastër. The demand for university places has remained consistently high, despite declining enrolment figures for secondary schools. Sadly though one of the prime motivations for seeking higher education among young people is to improve their chances of being able to emigrate.

Not safe for girls

While boys and girls have equal access to educational opportunities in the cities, there is a growing problem for girls getting secondary schooling in rural areas. Many children have to walk far distances to get to the nearest secondary school, and many parents have become reluctant to send their girls, due to the threat of girls being abducted and coerced into prostitution. The police have been relatively ineffective in controlling the continuing security problems in rural areas. Sotiraq Grozi, head teacher of the primary school in Voskopojë, is particularly concerned about this issue: 'Our students here are keen to learn, and their parents are very supportive of them getting an education. They finish school here when they are 14. I know that 80 per cent of the children here would like to attend secondary school in Korçë, but few of them will end up doing so. Besides, half of these students are girls, and because of the safety situation it is not possible for them to continue.' Public transport to the secondary school in Korçë would be a solution, 'but it needs money and the government to help us. The parents cannot pay themselves.' At the moment, primary school teachers come to Voskopojë by bus, and Sotiraq has tried to arrange for the same bus to take older students into Korçë to attend secondary school: 'However, the bus is owned by someone in Korçë and he does not want to accommodate us like this. We cannot afford our own bus service, so I am not sure how we will solve this problem. My daughter finishes at the school here this year and I don't know what to do because it is not safe for her to travel to Korçë. Many young girls have been abducted while they travel—they are not safe. If I had a boy then I would not worry so much.'

▲ *There is not much likelihood of these girls attending secondary school.*

'The future of our country is at stake': poverty and education

Sotiraq Grozi explains: 'It is really difficult for children in rural areas to get a proper education. Teachers work hard for ridiculously low salaries and with very little resources or support from the government. The children come from poor families who struggle to buy books and basic supplies. Fortunately, in this area the parents are really anxious for their children to get an education. Many families will make sacrifices to get their children the necessary books.'

While transport and safety problems make it difficult for the children of Voskopojë to go to secondary school in Korçë, Sotiraq knows that the situation is even worse in other regions. 'Distance is such a big problem in the north; there are too many kids not going to school. They are growing up without an education and are easily exposed to bad influences. I think that is why you see so much more crime among the youth in the north than here in the south: there is less of an emphasis on education.' Even in Voskopojë Commune, some villages are too far away for the children to have more than a basic primary education. But Sotiraq is quietly hopeful:

The village of Voskopojë has a rich educational and cultural history: in the 18th century, it was an important trade centre and home to the first university in the Balkans. The area is also rich in churches and at the height of its influence boasted 37 Greek Orthodox churches. With the decline of the Ottoman empire and the growth of Korçë, Voskopojë rapidly lost its influence; today, little remains of its former glory.

▲ *The children of Voskopojë playing outside their dilapidated primary school building.*

'There seem to be more problems to do with education in this country than there are answers. However, I try to be an optimist, and as long as we teachers work hard, there will be some sort of progress. If we work hard we can motivate our students. If we lose hope, then how will they ever have hope? We must not let this happen, because the future of our country is at stake.'

The effect of emigration

Voskopojë, like other villages in Albania, has seen an exodus of residents to Tiranë or Greece since the early 1990s; 50 out of 150 families have left. Sotiraq describes how this has affected schooling: 'We are losing more people every year. Normally, we have about 169 children in school, but at the moment there are only 89 students. The other children are with the families who are working in Greece. Because we have so few children we are having to combine the classes.'

Emigration does not necessarily mean an abrupt end to education: 'The children who go to Greece manage to continue their education there and do really well. They learn Greek quickly. There are also two children here who have been given scholarships to go to high school in Romania. Romania does a lot to help Albania like this, especially in this area which has some Vlach-speaking villages. Vlach is a language related to Romanian, and Romania does a lot to encourage ties and cultural exchanges because of this link.'

At the same time, children's awareness that they may have to leave Albania in order to make a living has changed their attitude to education. Sotiraq thinks that students were better motivated in the past: 'You knew that you were going to get a job when you finished your schooling. Now students are not motivated because there is no assistance to help them continue their education, and even if they did, there are no jobs to be had at the end of it. Consequently, once they get to about 14, all they think about is going to Greece. People are so poor now, and they don't have much opportunity in life; this makes it hard for them to have dreams and ambitions. Without dreams and ambitions, it is very difficult to find the motivation to keep studying.'

'We can now teach children to think for themselves'

Those Albanians who choose to work as teachers in spite of the low pay and bad conditions now take pride in their work, according to Sotiraq. 'There have been positive changes for us teachers: we feel more professional. In the old days it didn't matter whether you were a good teacher or not— you were just there to get the children to memorise things. We had to teach what the state wanted us to teach, so that the children would grow up as good communists. Now we have new materials to teach with, and we have a say in what we teach and how we teach it.' Although it is often very difficult to pay for new textbooks, teachers can use a greater variety of materials, and books are no longer censored. 'Teachers can develop their skills and ideas today, and therefore so can the students. We can teach children to think and reason for themselves, rather than just getting them to learn everything by heart like in the old days. We are not here to make robots. This is much more satisfying; it is what the profession of teaching should be all about.'

Albanian politicians need to concern themselves with the country's development so that these children will have jobs to go to after finishing their education.

The health system under pressure

One of the achievements of Albania's communist past was the availability of health care throughout the country. Primary health-care facilities could be found in even the most remote villages, and Albanians in both rural and urban areas had access to basic hospitals. Public sanitation and access to safe drinking water were dramatically improved; a vaccination programme was strictly adhered to, and with the arrival of electricity to every village in Albania by the mid-1970s, vaccines could safely be delivered to and kept cool in remote areas. (Even in the 1990s, Albania had a higher vaccination rate for certain diseases, for example measles, than some countries in the European Union.) The government forced doctors to serve in remote areas, and although they often worked in difficult conditions and lacked basic supplies and equipment, they were able to provide a minimum level of health care to Albania's predominantly rural population. Reductions in infant and child mortality led to a dramatic increase in life expectancy—from 54 years in 1950 to 72 years in 1985.

Staff in Korçë District hospital operate in theatres with only basic equipment.

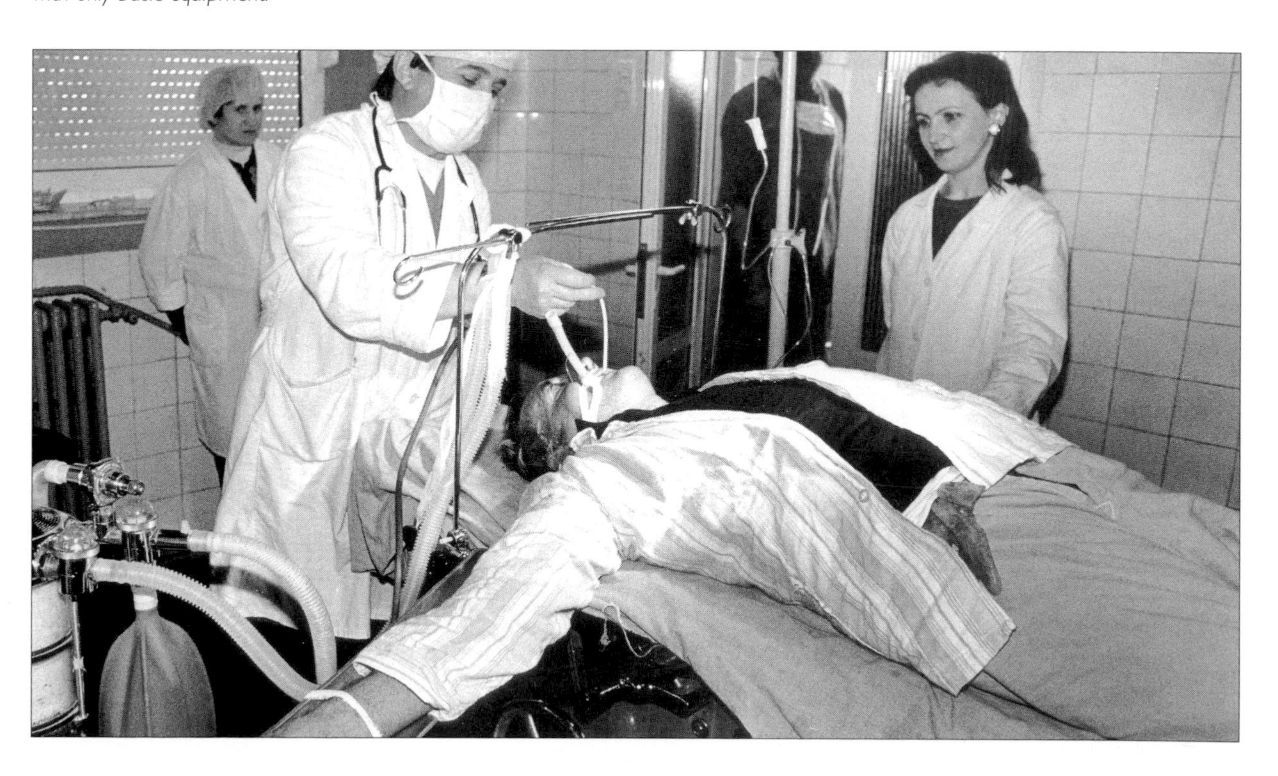

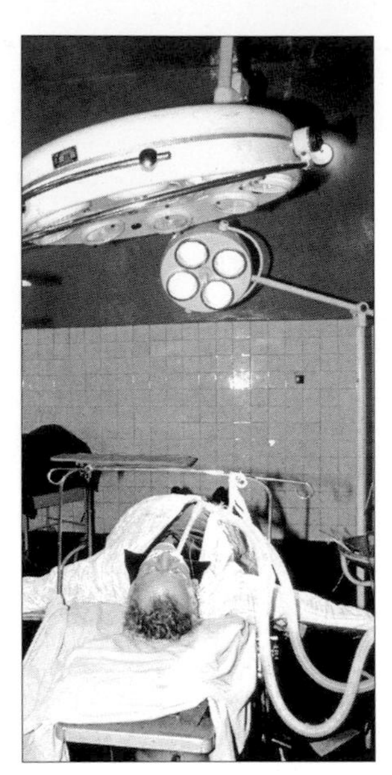

▲ *Albania only has 50 hospitals left, less than one-third of the pre-1991 number.*

Yet in the past 15 years these once impressive achievements have paled in significance. By 1985 Albania's isolation and increasingly fragile economy had begun to erode the quality of health care in the country. Doctors increasingly worked without even the most basic of medicines. As shortages of food became more and more common, people's nutrition levels declined. Hygiene and sanitation became more of a problem as water supply and sewerage started to break down, and shortages of articles such as soap became a regular occurrence. Incidences of malnutrition started to appear, especially in the more remote parts of the north of the country. The state supplied drugs without expiration dates, so doctors were often forced to work with medicines that had probably expired—when they could get them.

The consequences of economic adjustment

After the fall of communism and during the chaos of 1991–92, the health service went through a serious crisis. Many facilities, especially in rural areas, were looted and damaged, and staff fled in fear to the relative security of towns and cities. There has been a continuous 'brain drain' of medical professionals through emigration, and it is increasingly difficult to find doctors and nurses willing to work in the more remote rural areas. Given doctors' remarkably low salaries ($100 a month in many cases), an informal market in health care has developed where patients have to pay doctors for treatments and operations. Hospital patients are often expected to provide their own food and medicines.

Due to restraints on public spending, imposed as part of IMF and World Bank structural adjustment packages, hundreds of smaller rural health centres have been closed in recent years. This has left a significant proportion of the population without access to adequate health-care facilities; average travel times to the nearest facility can be anywhere from two hours to two days in the most remote mountainous areas of the north. In 1991 there were 160 hospitals; two years later only 50 remained, only three of which were located in villages. The far-reaching network of maternity clinics established under communism has shared the same fate, as is reflected in the increase in mother and infant deaths since 1991. Figures for infant mortality by 1994 were already 2.5 times higher than the 1992 rate for all industrialised countries. Maternal mortality rates have shown similar increases: by 1994, they had climbed to more than three times the 1988 average for the European Community. Despite concentrated efforts by the Albanian government and foreign donors, these rates have remained constant, although it is hoped that the effects of new investment in the health sector will reduce levels of infant and maternal mortality in the near future.

Despite these problems, the effectiveness of Albania's vaccination programme has been maintained, one of the positive effects of significant international assistance since 1990. Life expectancy has remained high, although there have been many deaths and disabilities related to automobile accidents as a result of the phenomenal increase in the number of private motor vehicles, which were banned before 1991.

Abortion, which was illegal under communist rule except for medical reasons, has seen a significant increase as Albanian society has become slightly more permissive, especially in urban areas. Although abortion is now legal its cost, and unsafe practices by some doctors keen to bolster their meagre incomes, have led to an increase in abortion-related deaths. Contraception has not really taken root in Albanian society, despite the increase in promiscuity of young men and women: just over 2 per cent of women were using contraceptive methods in 1997. Traditional attitudes to contraception, particularly among young men, will impede its widespread use.

The situation since 1997

The protests and violence of 1997 placed an enormous additional burden on the already seriously weakened health service. Medical staff describe situations akin to military field hospitals as they tried to deal with the thousands of Albanians killed or injured during the civil unrest. Unable to cope, most hospitals, particularly in the south, acted as first aid stations from where patients were flown to Greece by helicopter for more extensive treatment. According to one nurse in Korçë, 'it was like a war zone, with armed men bringing in dozens of wounded people and threatening us to work on this patient or that patient. All we could do was patch them up and put them on the helicopter to Greece.'

While some significant improvements have been made in Albania's standards of health care since 1997, particularly in urban areas, much still remains to be done. Standards are still declining dramatically in rural areas, as the difficulty of finding doctors and nurses willing to work in these areas increases. Access to safe water and proper sanitation are still under significant threat, and in many rural areas, especially in the mountainous north, villagers have to walk up to three hours in order to find safe drinking water. In shanty towns like Kamza near Tiranë, the lack of essential public health infrastructure poses the threat of a major public health epidemic. As thousands of impoverished northerners continue to flock to these areas in search of a better life, such risks increase by the day.

However, with sustained international aid going to Albania's health sector, health care in Albania can once more become one of the country's strongest assets. If the efforts of hundreds of dedicated Albanian doctors and nurses working under incredibly difficult conditions are anything to go by, then such hopes will surely become reality.

In many remote villages, people still fetch water from sources such as springs located deep inside mountain caves.

'We are doing a very difficult job'

Korçë District Hospital in the south of Albania serves four districts: Ersekë, Korçë, Devoll and Pogradec. Vera Pupa has worked there for 30 years, 20 of which as the Head Nurse in the Intensive Care Unit. For her, 1997 and 1998 were especially difficult years, because of the violence and the associated rise in emergency cases with gun wounds. But Vera can identify some positive aspects: 'Although this was a terrible time for us, we learned a lot from it. In the past, 95 per cent of our operations were planned, and we had very few genuine emergency cases. But during 1997, we had to respond immediately to save people's lives and work under the most severe pressure. It was very stressful, but we all worked hard and were able to save hundreds of people.' Knowing that they can cope under such terrible circumstances has given health staff renewed confidence: 'Although our health system is poor in terms of equipment, this period proved that we have good training and skills, and above all, that we are compassionate. As a team, we all had great spirit and supported each other. We all found it very frightening: people would come in with guns and threaten us in order to make us look after this person immediately. It is very hard to reason with such people and remain calm; we just had to keep telling them that we were doing our best, and fortunately, nobody got hurt. The Greek hospitals helped us a lot during this time by taking patients once we had provided the necessary emergency treatment.'

Stringent public-sector reform has certainly changed the way Korçë District Hospital is managed, according to Vera: 'We make better use of the limited resources we have. Although some aspects of health care were better during communism, it was also very wasteful and inefficient. People were not accountable for their work or the materials they were entrusted with. There is still a lot of work to be done, but because of the new attitudes in administration and management, there is much more of a spirit of co-operation and teamwork here. We need this to help our patients as much as possible.'

But political and economic reform has also changed social attitudes in Albania: 'The public tends to treat this hospital like a bus station. They come in and out of here as they please, which they never used to do. People tend to be very aggressive; they don't respect that this is a hospital and that we are doing a very difficult job.' This behaviour is made worse by the economic situation: 'Because so many people don't have jobs, a patient often has 20 visitors at once—they have nothing else to do. In a ward of ten beds, there can be 200 people visiting; how are we supposed to work in such an environment?' Vera thinks that something can be done to improve the situation: 'People who have worked in Greece behave much better, because they have seen how a

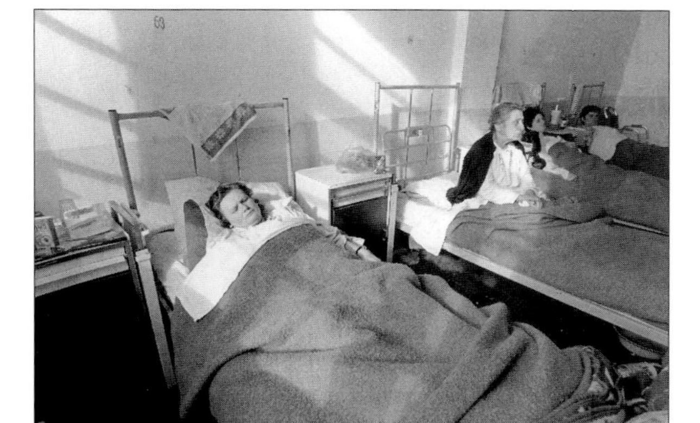

▼ *A typical ward—but without visitors.*

▲ *Vera Pupa describes the challenges facing Albanian doctors and nurses.*

modern hospital should work. We need to educate people better about health issues. Also, if there were more jobs, fewer people would just hang around visiting patients.'

Vera manages to balance her own worries with the understanding that rebuilding the health-care system is an immense task: 'I love my job even though the conditions are very difficult. I hope our salaries will increase, not because I am greedy but because it is very hard to survive and feed my family on what I earn. Also, we are losing a lot of doctors through emigration because the salaries are so low. The government is trying to solve this problem, but it will need a lot of help from foreign countries. In the meantime we must just keep working hard. At least we are satisfied knowing that we are managing to help people.'

New concepts and freedoms

One of the most striking aspects of Albania's transition to democracy has been the variety of ways in which individuals have reacted to a climate free of many of the restrictions of the communist period. The ineffectiveness of state institutions and a general disregard for authority have led to incidents of anarchy in the last few years, as Albanians' frustration at their continuing economic hardship and the lack of opportunities has manifested itself in violence. However, this violence has been a collective expression of individual anger, rather than an organised and unified force for change. But while on most occasions since the fall of communism when Albanians acted together, this action was associated with violence and anarchy, a young, dynamic NGO sector has sprung up at the same time.

Prior to 1990 there were no NGOs whatsoever in Albania, and the country lacks a tradition of non-governmental activity. All activities were organised and sponsored by the state, which has left Albania without a cultural framework in which to develop a civil society. In spite of this, remarkable progress has been achieved by a small number of local NGOs, particularly by women's organisations.

Restoring a sense of community

Given the sudden change from extreme social collectivisation to extreme individualism, many NGOs have found it hard to establish themselves. Social action is still perceived very much as part of the previous system's enforced voluntary work ethic. The result of 50 years of communist rule has been a weakened sense of community in Albania, and an inherent mistrust of any agenda that promotes equality. Many Albanian NGOs see their role as rebuilding a sense of community. Sonila Qirjaku, the Director of the Albanian Women's Centre, describes the challenge: 'Volunteerism was a dirty word in the old system, and people are still left with this mentality. We have to find ways of getting people to participate and be active without them necessarily seeing it as voluntary work.'

▼ Sonila Qirjaku hopes to overcome Albanians' suspicion of working together.

The events of 1997 were a watershed for local NGOs, as public opinion began to accept their role in a new Albanian society. As the state institutions ceased to function, local NGOs were able to fill in the gaps rapidly and provide much-needed assistance to thousands of Albanians. Although a similar crisis occurred in 1991–92, foreign organisations were the main source of assistance at the time. Albanians were impressed to see

An NGO near Shkodër aims to improve rural communications by producing and distributing a newsletter.

that in 1997 it was local organisations which were the most visible in responding to the crisis, despite serious security concerns. One of the most positive images of 1997 was a demonstration for peace in Tiranë at the height of the troubles, organised by local NGOs and led by a coalition of women's groups. Many people joined the demonstration as it wound its way through Tiranë, and this demonstration of solidarity amid chaos made a big impression on Albanians. People saw it as a message of hope and recognised NGOs as an important force in a new Albania.

Challenges ahead

Nevertheless, Albania's fledgling NGO movement has many challenges to overcome in order to build on its achievements to date. Sonila Qirjaku of the Albanian Women's Centre lists one of them: 'There is still too much competition among NGOs; a lot of it is politically motivated, and the old mentalities do not help in resolving this. In our case, co-operation with the political women's organisations continues to be a problem. As NGOs we can't work with them openly, but they do represent a lot of women, so we have to develop some form of working relationship. This is also important because they can be very useful to us at the political level in lobbying and influencing government.'

But working together to achieve change is still proving difficult, because individual NGOs do not always see the advantage of co-operation. Mirela Jonuzaj, Director of the Albanian Disability Rights Foundation (ADREF) feels that this is a particular problem among NGOs working on disability issues: 'All too often people see setting an NGO up as a means of getting money, power and influence. They need to develop a long-term view of their future and see that we are all working together for the rights of all disabled people, not just the blind, for example.'

Most Albanian NGOs are based in Tiranë, and many have problems expanding their activities beyond the capital. As Sonila points out, 'there are 65 women's NGOs in this country, but only seven of these are not from Tiranë. Of the supposedly "national" NGOs, only six or seven have branches in the Districts, and very few of these are active. We need to develop and expand our membership bases outside Tiranë if we are to reach rural people, particularly women.' Sonila Qirjaku also highlights the need to improve the management structures of local NGOs: 'There is a need to develop the leadership skills of younger people as many organisations are dominated by intellectuals whose management experience is rooted in the communist past.'

Because there are hardly any local sources of funding, most Albanian organisations are completely reliant on donor funding. Albanian NGOs have recently managed to get a special dispensation for income-generation projects from the government, with which they can finance their activities. Although foreign funding for NGOs in Albania has increased, the capacity of many local NGOs to absorb much of this funding is still very weak. This strengthens many local groups' belief that Western donors are imposing their model of development, and that they are not free to develop more appropriate and effective solutions to local problems. Improved dialogue between local NGOs and the donor community can help to resolve this in the future.

Despite the many obstacles that NGOs in Albania are faced with, they are becoming increasingly effective and important players in shaping a new society. Local organisations were instrumental in helping the government draft the country's first post-communist constitution, as well as in raising public awareness of electoral processes. They have tackled the question of security by holding local discussions on the collection of weapons. NGOs aim to help Albanians cope without the safety-net of a controlling state, and provide a widely-needed service network. Their activities include offering family planning and parenting advice; giving out information on drug and alcohol abuse; counselling women on issues of violence, health, and the law; by arranging legal representation for disadvantaged women; making and supplying wheelchairs for handicapped persons; and by providing training and support services to business entrepreneurs and managers.

Albanian women's struggle for equality

The women's movement in Albania has probably seen the most dramatic developments of any sector of Albanian society since 1991. Women have been at the forefront of social change, and women's NGOs are among the most progressive and active in Albania. While much remains to be done in terms of women's rights and their equal participation in Albanian society, a very solid foundation for change has been built in the past eight years.

Under communist rule, much progress was made in terms of promoting equal opportunities for women. The communist period was effective in forcing a highly traditional, conservative, and patriarchal Albanian society to accept women playing an active role in everyday social life; however, because women's emancipation was part of the ideological doctrines of Marxism-Leninism, this emancipation was limited to their activities outside the home. Attitudes towards women's and men's roles in the household remained relatively unchanged. As a consequence, Albanian women felt free when outside, but subdued within the confines of their homes. The arrival of democracy allowed women to engage actively in challenging such attitudes, while at the same time struggling to safeguard the limited rights and equalities they had gained during communism.

Albania's transition to a democracy has unquestionably given Albanian women more freedom. But reforms have also brought new challenges: the large-scale closure of thousands of state enterprises and the scaling-down of government bureaucracies have caused high unemployment among women. Women were the first to lose their jobs, and have become more dependent upon their husbands as a result. Because a greater proportion of women now stay at home—in contrast to the years of communist rule—many women feel detached from active participation in Albanian social life and politics.

▼ *Many women contribute to the family income, but they are still struggling to attain equal status within the family.*

Other economic changes have been felt most by rural women. Since the redistribution of land, subsistence and small-scale commercial agriculture has developed in rural areas. Most land units are too small to justify the purchase of agricultural machinery, even if families can afford it. With the high rate of emigration of men to Greece and Italy, rural women increasingly have to spend most of their time working the land, with the most primitive of means. The daily manual labour that rural women must carry out in order to ensure their families' survival leaves them little or no time to participate in any other activities.

▲ *Joane Joshari, who is 16 years old, has recently started work in a textile factory in Korçë.*

Younger women in both rural and urban areas, but particularly in rural areas, have become increasingly concerned about the poor levels of personal security for women, and this has greatly restricted their movement and participation in daily life outside the home. The situation for women in cities, particularly Tiranë, is looking up because foreign companies and the growing service sector have created job opportunities. Nevertheless many women still work in jobs that pay little and require a minimum of formal training or skills.

Prostitution

Ironically, villages and small cities have become primary sources for the growing trade in prostitution in Albania—despite their more traditional and conservative attitudes. According to Afroviti Gushto, who works for the women's NGO Reflexione in Pogradec, this is because 'these girls are too naïve, as are their parents. The parents, and especially the father, are often without work. The boys who encourage the girls into prostitution tell the parents that the girls are simply going away to work in hotels or "honourable" professions. The lure of the money that the girls will earn helps further to convince poor families. It then becomes really difficult for the girls who feel that they have nobody to turn to, as even their families are pressuring them to go.' Reflexione wants to address this problem by educating girls in a new counselling centre: 'It may be dangerous because certain men involved with the mafia are making a lot of money out of this trade and they will not want us doing this, but for me it is the biggest problem concerning women's human rights in this country. We must start doing something before it gets completely out of hand.'

▼ *Silva Fulani, who counsels women fleeing violent situations.*

Silva Fulani of the LINEA Counselling Centre and Shelter in Tiranë is also concerned with the problem of prostitution and its effect on young women in rural areas. 'Prostitution is a very sensitive and difficult issue in Albania. We see women who are trying to escape from prostitution and look on our shelter as a means of refuge. However, we must develop programmes that can help such women with the difficult process of re-integrating back into a normal life. For girls from rural areas, the problem of prostitution is made worse by their lack of education and naïvety. They are easily swayed by the boys who try to trick them into it with promises of money and nice clothes, and an escape from the drudgery of their lives at home.'

Divorce and domestic violence

Albania is still very much a patriarchal society, and attitudes towards a variety of issues such as domestic violence and divorce remain deeply conservative even in urban areas. As Silva Fulani points out, 'a lot of women accept violence against them as normal, because wives are traditionally subservient to their husbands in Albania. Many women consider emotional and psychological abuse as a normal part of married life. It is very hard for them to distinguish between what they see as their duties as a wife and what is abuse. For example, a young woman told us the other day that her fiancé won't let her out of the house alone. We are a Mediterranean people with strong emotions and passions, but this makes it very difficult for some to distinguish between passion and emotional violence. Men feel that they have to put some limits on their women's freedom in order to demonstrate that they care. It is very difficult to change such a mentality in both men and women.'

The issue of divorce is a more recent problem. Under communism, the state would only allow divorce on grounds of adultery; in other cases, it would interfere and try to resolve conflicts between husbands and wives. The Party favoured a strong family concept and did not want to be seen to be encouraging divorce. Divorce could damage one's career—especially a woman's career—and it carried a social stigma. The new freedoms have brought an increase in the number of divorces, but other factors limit women's choice, as Silva explains. 'Many women have no means of financial support and as a result, although their marriages are a complete failure, women don't know where to turn and feel very trapped.' Silva's organisation, LINEA, helps women by talking through a woman's options with her, offering legal advice, as well as a place of shelter should the woman decide to leave home. 'We are not openly encouraging divorce, but we are concerned at the level of violence and abuse in such situations, and how this will affect the children of such a marriage. With so many men unemployed, frustrated, bored and with nothing else to do but drink, I worry that the problem of violence in the home is going to get worse rather than better in the near future.'

▼ *Women's NGOs hope to increase girls' chances of leading unconstrained lives and making their own choices.*

LINEA also runs a counselling centre in Shkodër in the north of the country, which has helped the organisation gain a better understanding of the problems women face in parts of Albania which are less cosmopolitan and open-minded than the capital. Lida of the Shkodër centre explains: 'Shkodër is very different to Tiranë. It is a provincial town with strong ties to the very traditional rural areas that surround it. It is a small town, and everyone knows everyone else. People believe that problems should be solved within the family.'

Lida feels that the public awareness work the Shkodër centre is undertaking about issues of domestic violence and women's rights is essential. 'It is important that women do not just accept violence as so many have traditionally done. We must break the silence of women in Albania on such issues and change the mentality that women are seen and treated like property.' By being sensitive to local traditions, LINEA workers try to minimise hostility to change: 'The public education work has gained us a lot of support. We try to reassure people that we are here to help families resolve their problems and only see divorce as a last resort. It is also important that we are seen as professional counsellors and not as trying to push things from a feminist perspective. There is no tradition of this here yet, and it only serves to confuse people and make them suspicious towards us, especially men.' Working in a part of Albania that has a tradition of violence can be tough, as Lida describes. 'We often get husbands phoning and threatening us, which can be frightening. Nevertheless, we try to sensitise other family members to get the husband to see reason and accept that his behaviour towards his wife is intolerable.'

Sonila Qirjaku of the Women's Centre in Tiranë also highlights the need for a flexible, evolutionary approach to working with women in rural areas. 'If we don't try to understand what life is like for women in rural areas, we will be seen as ridiculing them, which will further erode their self-esteem. The best way to start working with rural women is through encouraging them to see women's issues as those of the family, rather than their own immediate problems. I think that given the traditional and conservative nature of a lot of our rural areas, you have to go through the back door rather than the front door in order to address women's rights.'

Legal changes

The process of drafting Albania's new constitution had significant input from various women's organisations. According to Milva Ekonomi, President of Reflexione in Pogradec, the constitution represents a positive framework for ensuring women's equality in Albania. However, like many others she is concerned that the continuing lack of law and order will make enforcement of many aspects of the new constitution difficult. She also feels that women in southern Albania are likely to experience emancipation sooner than women in the north. 'Women in the north are more reserved than those in the south, and the traditions and customs they are

The virginesh tradition

An ancient tradition in Albania's rural areas would ensure that no household was left without a male head of the family. If the only adult man in a family died or was killed in a blood feud, an unmarried woman could 'become' a man in order to ensure that her family was represented at village council meetings. Assuming male clothes, social status, work duties, and—with time—male behaviour and looks, this *virginesh* would continue her life as a man, maintaining the social order. In some rare instances, this tradition can still be found today.

Lulë from Vukaj, a village near Shkodër, chose to be a *virginesh* in 1968 (at the height of the communist cultural revolution) because she did not want to marry the man her family had chosen for her. Since then, she has worked as a farmer and teacher.

faced with are so much stronger and repressive. In addition, access to infrastructure like education and transport is so much worse in the north, especially for women.'

Silva Fulani also emphasises that having laws that protect women's rights is only the first step: 'We still have a long way to go. The attitude of the police, for example to domestic violence, is hopeless. There are no female police officers, and male officers are often highly unsympathetic. If a woman goes to the police to report a case of violence against her by her husband, then it must go to court. Naturally women are very uncomfortable with going public; they don't want to go to the police and risk splitting up the family.' Although a new law was passed which gives women the right to say whether or not the case should go to court, most women are unaware of such changes in the law. Silva concludes, 'they are protected on paper but not in practice', but hopes that public awareness campaigns, aimed at both men and women, will remedy this.

Given the many challenges facing Albanian women, progress has been made regarding all aspects of women's rights. Much still remains to be done, but with an active and effective women's NGO community continuing advancement of women's equality seems assured, and, as Sonila Qirjaku points out: 'the state no longer sees the women's movement as opponents but more as partners. There have been a lot of successful partnerships between women's groups and the government in the last few years. Our opinions are becoming increasingly important, and I think that women are going to play an increasingly important and equal part in shaping a new Albanian society in the years to come.'

Unlocking the doors: the challenges facing people with disabilities

Under communism, disability was seen as a medical rather than a social issue, so little, if any, effort was made to enable disabled people to play an active role in society. However, a generous benefits system was in place to meet their basic needs. Because of widespread ignorance about disability, hundreds of Albanians were institutionalised or did not receive adequate medical assistance, and traditional views of disability resulted in many families feeling a sense of shame and many children being hidden away or put in institutions. Such cultural perceptions of disability are still widespread throughout Albania today. However, the arrival of democracy and greater freedom has had both positive and negative consequences for

▼ Lunturi, Buiar, and Afrodite Dojka, who suffer from paralysis, with their mother Bihana outside their home in a small village south of Tiranë. Despite the Dojkas' financial straits, the three benefit from their family's loving care.

disabled people in Albania. It has stripped away much of the social safety net for many disabled people, leaving them confused and economically vulnerable. At the same time, many people with disabilities have grasped the opportunity to challenge cultural attitudes and actively pursue their rights, which have so long been denied to them.

In the early years of Albania's transformation, the rest of the world was shocked by horrific images of institutions for the mentally handicapped in Albania. While the conditions and care available in such facilities have improved dramatically, much remains to be done to convince people that community care and integration are viable alternatives to isolation and institutionalisation. The country's poor infrastructure presents a huge physical barrier for many disabled people to overcome: hundreds of people are stuck in fifth-floor apartments without wheelchairs or lifts. It is not uncommon to meet disabled people who have not left their apartments for several years at a time. Even if they are able to get outside, the potholes, crumbling sidewalks with numerous deep uncovered manholes, and an abundance of reckless drivers make moving around a daunting prospect for disabled people. Hardly any buildings in Albania have disabled access.

Despite such overwhelming obstacles, disabled people in Albania are becoming increasingly active and assertive of their rights. An NGO-run project to build wheelchairs specifically designed for Albania's challenging physical environment has been set up; it is reaching hundreds of disabled people throughout the country who had been restricted to their beds for years. With a corresponding programme of rehabilitation and public education, disabled people are gaining much greater visibility in Albanian daily life. A national organisation representing all aspects of disability, the Albanian Disability Rights Foundation (ADREF), is challenging traditional perceptions and stereotypes of disability and has been involved in drafting legislation for the new constitution, to secure the rights of disabled people.

The road ahead

Significant challenges lie ahead. The disability movement consists of many organisations specific to a certain form of disability such as blindness, paraplegia or mental disability. Many organisations have found it hard to relate to the lack of state funding and the new climate of self-help in Albania. The legacy of communism has also made it difficult for a climate of sufficient trust to develop which would enable such organisations to work together for the rights of disabled people as a group. As Mirela Jonuzaj of ADREF says: 'We are working hard to provide training to local NGOs. Disabled people are still not very visible in everyday life in Albania. The wheelchair project now being run by ADREF after initial help from Oxfam has been a very positive project in this respect. It has also given us a lot of credibility with the government as we have something tangible and concrete to show them. When we go to the Government to try to get proper legislation, they can see that we have achieved things on our own and are serious. The wheelchair project has also got us a lot of media attention around the country and served as a useful platform for wider education work about disability issues.'

Mirela also feels that disabled people themselves have to change their attitude. 'Disabled people have had many problems and obstacles to overcome. Often this has left them with a very negative view of society and of themselves. If you don't care about yourself and see everything as useless, how can you expect public opinion to change?' Mirela understands that disabled people have had little chance to explore their own talents, but she has an example of what is possible. 'Cimi, one of our beneficiaries, used to stay in bed and suffer from depression before he got his wheelchair. At first he was ashamed to go out into the street and be seen in public. We were able to give him a lot of encouragement, and now he is incredibly active and a great source of inspiration to other wheelchair users. He is involved in all our activities and was instrumental in starting Albania's first wheelchair basketball team. He has travelled all over the country with them, and they recently played some matches in Romania. When people see Cimi they become really motivated. They start to believe that if they themselves change then they can change society.'

The rapid pace of change in Albania since 1991 has left many disabled people bewildered, frustrated and confused. For many people with disabilities, the meagre state assistance they receive has left them on the margins of survival and with a sense of hopelessness. Coupled with traditional negative attitudes towards disability, it will be difficult for many disabled people to reverse this trend of alienation and apathy. However, the work of organisations like ADREF and the determination of many disabled people to be included as full participants in Albanian society, will help to overcome many of these barriers.

'I feel part of what is happening in this town'

Pallumb Guri has had Multiple Sclerosis since he was a child. He is a recognised poet, with two volumes of poetry already published. Pallumb has only recently acquired a wheelchair, but is an active person well-known in his home town, Lushnjë. He recently got permission and funding to start Lushnjë's second private radio station—it will just take some more paperwork: 'There is still no law on private media, so this is still all a bit confusing, and sometimes we worry about censorship. There is a private TV station here, but they don't have a news programme because they are skeptical about guarantees of freedom of speech for private media, especially as the previous government tried to control all forms of media. However, I want to have a radio programme on the life of disabled people in Albania and their issues and difficulties. I also want the station to devote some time to art and culture, which is very important in Albania if we are to move forward, and also to take our minds off all the bad things that have happened. A society without art and culture cannot develop.'

▲ *Pallumb Guri, poet and radio entrepreneur, in his local bar in Lushnjë.*

Pallumb is a keen observer of life in Albania, and feels the need to comment on what is happening: 'I have been writing for ten years. I write about many things, but I also try to write about those things that a lot of people don't have the courage to write about. I want people to see that I don't just write based on my experience as a disabled person. I see the negative things that are happening in our country and feel I must talk about them. In my last book I wrote about a girl who was a good friend of mine when I was a child. I hear she has gone to Italy as a prostitute. I find this very sad and want people to know that we must try and stop such tragedies. Although it makes me tired sometimes, I always have the energy to write. There is so much going on in this country right now that people need to think about!'

Pallumb started to write as a means of keeping depression at bay. 'When I was a child I was unable to go to school because of my disability. I managed to make friends, but I felt sad when they went to school and I was left alone. I have tried to fill this gap by painting and writing poetry. I did not have a wheelchair so I could not get around; and being trapped in my apartment affected my physical development. I could have been a lot stronger than I am now if I had had a wheelchair to move around and use my muscles.'

Pallumb has been supporting people with disabilities or other difficulties: 'I believe that we are equal even though we may have different problems.' Now that he has a wheelchair, he can be even more active. 'I have a lot of friends, and now I am able to go out with them in town. I go out every day and feel a part of what is happening in this town. As a result, people don't treat me as though I'm disabled. I hope to move from my apartment, which is on the fifth floor, so that I can get out and about on my own. I am very demanding of life and cannot live a single day without doing something.'

Pallumb sometimes feels sorry that many Albanians of his age are so keen to leave. 'I have many friends who have gone to Tiranë or moved abroad. I miss them and sometimes feel like I wish to leave. However, I was born here and I grew up here, and this is the place where I have found my identity. That is why I want to stay, and I want to tell this to people who are leaving: that they should stay and do something for the next generation.'

This concern for Albania's future is a great part of Pallumb's motivation to write and communicate. 'I hope that people everywhere can relate to my poetry and see me as a poet first, looking beyond my disability. People have a bad image of Albania, which makes me sad. I want to tell the world that we are a good and sensitive people. We have our bad people just like any country, but they are only a minority. The rest of us just want to work hard and care for each other.'

THE SEA IS OF TEARS

The taste of tears you have the sea
That is why I say the sea is of tears.

If you gather all the tears of Albanian mothers
And the tears of all the mothers of the world
The sea is of tears.

And people still do not understand the causes of human suffering
Which God will come and take on the sins of this dirty world
Just tell me when.

Pallumb Guri

The environment: too little, too late?

Albania's transformation into an industrialised country was achieved with little regard to the environment. Fulfilling the communist government's ambitious production targets were the only concern, at a terrible cost to the environment. Today Albania is littered with the remnants of this industrial legacy. Of the factories still working, many are only working at 20 per cent or less of their former capacity. Working with outdated Chinese technology and without any environmental protection measures, these factories serve as grim reminders of the past. The transition to democracy has also provided very little effective legislation for environmental protection, and consequently, many decrepit factories continue to pump out pollutants.

A pall of grey-brown smog obscures the horizon around the massive steelworks in Elbasan in central Albania, while in Laç near the coast women reported that after a few days' wear their nylon stocking would melt from the clouds of smoke hanging over the city from the fertiliser

▼ *Hoxha's investment in heavy industry has left a harmful legacy for Albanians.*

plant. Perhaps the most alarming example of industrial pollution is the maze of oil fields in the south of the country, especially around Ballsh. Decrepit oil rigs pump out black sludge over neighbouring fields, and the rivers and streams run black with raw crude oil, while children play around miniature lakes of oil.

Widespread industrial pollution is not the only environmental hazard threatening Albania at the moment. Deforestation and resulting soil erosion are a pressing problem throughout the country. With the breakdown of law and order since the fall of communism, people living in mountain villages have been able to cut down trees in protected state lands for firewood. The deforestation of thousands of acres of hillside is truly alarming, and it has been compounded by the overgrazing of such hillsides by sheep, whose numbers have exploded since 1991. The silting of Albania's many rivers has also been a noticeable phenomenon in recent years, which has further compounded water and electricity shortages.

In the towns and cities, former green areas have been taken over by kiosks and stalls from the thousands of small businesses that have

▼ *The oil fields of central Albania make hazardous children's playgrounds.*

mushroomed since 1991. Despite the city councils' efforts, garbage dumps surround apartment blocks and remain uncollected for weeks at a time. Many of the thousands of cars that are being brought into the country—often illegally—are poorly maintained diesels, belching fumes into the air and enveloping most cities in a haze of smog that can be seen for miles.

Public awareness

Public awareness of environmental issues and the effects of pollution is very low in Albania. In the past five years, a number of NGOs working in this area have developed in Albania, which see it as their primary purpose to alert Albanians to the risks and dangers that they have inherited from 50 years of neglect. These NGOs are also working with the government to help draft the country's first environmental action plan.

According to Mihallaq Qirjo of the Regional Environmental Centre, this is an ongoing struggle: environmental protection is still low on the list of national priorities, and it is even worse at the local government level. 'Other daily issues like economic survival and security are so important. In a questionnaire we did in 1998, both the government and the public ranked environmental concerns tenth on a list of problems. People here don't really have an understanding of wider environmental issues—they tend to see them in terms of everyday problems, for example the amount of rubbish in the streets.' Mihallaq also links this lack of concern to Albanians' desire to finally *not* do as they are told: 'With all the new freedoms they feel they have a right to use the environment as they see fit without thought for the consequences. They still think that looking after the environment is the state's responsibility. Everyone sees the environment purely as an economic concern. There have been numerous proposals put forward for environmental protection, but many of them end up being blocked by the Ministry of Finance because of their negative economic implications. The environment is not yet a political issue and until it becomes one, it will be very difficult to effect change.'

Nevertheless, environmental legislation is slowly being put in place. Once standards have been set, the political will to monitor—and, if necessary, close down—environmentally hazardous activities will be crucial. Creating jobs will be the government's top priority for years to come, so a genuine commitment to protecting the environment is unlikely. The weak law and order situation and a lack of resources throughout the country will also make implementation difficult. Therefore local NGOs' efforts to raise public consciousness on such issues must play a large part in solving this problem.

Industrial pollution

The countryside around Ballsh presents some of the most disturbing images of industrial pollution in Albania. The area is rich in oil, and thousands of oil rigs dot the landscape. Unfortunately, most of these state-owned wells are no longer maintained, and the rigs spew oil over fields and into rivers. The people of the area used to be dependent on the nearby refinery for their livelihoods. Now without work, they are angry and confused as they try to earn a living from their damaged lands. In the village of Visokë, some people are trying to get the government to accept responsibility for the damage done over the past 50 years.

▼ Kazim Cella is determined not to put up with the effects of environmental damage.

Standing next to a rig whose spilling oil has damaged her family's land and crops, Behia Cella says: 'We don't have access to drinking water anymore, because some of the wells have filled up with oil. The animals often get sick from drinking the water, and then we can't eat them. Even people get sick from it. The government keeps saying that they will clean up the water, but so far they have done nothing.' Her husband Kazim Cella adds: 'The people come from the factory once a day to check this oil well, but they are too lazy to do anything. They don't cap it or try to stop it pouring oil all over the place. They just look at it and drive away again.'

Kazim worked for the oil company for 20 years and knows how much money is wasted by allowing oil to gush out freely. 'I lost my job at the oil company, and it has damaged my land, but I get no compensation. Each year the land produces less and less—everyone here is affected.' So far, the new democratic Albania has not delivered change in Visokë: 'There is supposed to be a law that says we should be compensated, but so far we have seen nothing. The oil company also promised us that they would come and drill some new water wells to replace our polluted ones, but so far they have done nothing. The doctors tell us not to drink the water, but what are we supposed to do? There is so much water here, but we are only

▶ *The crude oil sludge that is destroying farmers' livelihoods around Visokë.*

supposed to look at it, not drink it.' Kazim, Behia and others tried to improve the situation by sending a petition to the government. 'The government then ordered the oil company to come and drill the wells, but ordering them to do it and actually making them do it are two different things.' In addition, they also encountered censure for taking action: 'When we signed the petition, some people in the village were angry with us. Everyone used to work for the oil company, and they felt that if we criticised the oil company, they would not give us jobs when it started working again. Some of these people tried to stop us sending the petition—but we cannot continue like this.'

'Europe's wild west': the breakdown of law and order

During March 1997—with the government in a state of collapse and riots all over the country as a result of millions of Albanians losing their life savings in the collapse of the pyramid investment schemes—the police and army ceased to function. Faced with mobs of angry protesters, many police simply took off their uniforms and went home or joined the crowds. Poorly trained and equipped young soldiers, who had no wish to fire on their fellow Albanians, deserted army units in droves. Police stations and army weapons depots were left unguarded and stormed by civilians, who proceeded to take whatever weapons they could find. About 656,000 guns (from small pistols to anti-tank weapons), 3.5 million handgrenades, and 1 million land mines were stolen; in some cases, angry crowds even seized tanks. The resulting anarchy and the wealth of weaponry in civilian hands led to a complete breakdown in law and order. Finally, an international peace-keeping force arrived in April to attempt to restore a sense of order and begin the long and painful process of disarming the civilian population.

Although some degree of order has since been restored, there is still an enormous amount of weapons in civilian hands. The past three years have seen a dramatic increase in crime in Albania, and the role of organised crime is apparent. The police still remain relatively ineffective amid allegations that they are aiding and abetting the Albanian mafia. The absence of law and order during 1997 was compounded by deepening economic hardship, the uncontrolled migration of rural dwellers, particularly from the north, to the cities, and a failure to understand that freedom is a function of law, contributing to Albania's growing social problems. The illegal occupation of land by people moving from villages to cities gave rise to conflicts between the newcomers and legitimate owners. The tradition of blood feuds in northern Albania revived to fill the power vacuum. Encouraged by the ready availability of guns, the north saw violent conclusions of many old and new family vendettas. In some areas, the blood feuding between families has got so bad that entire generations of men are prisoners in their own homes. The police have proved particularly reluctant to become involved in such disputes, arguing that they are family matters and impossible to resolve; but of course the police are also afraid of becoming part of the vendetta.

It is a sad statistic that the most common crimes in Albania in 1997, according to the UNDP, were murder (50 per cent of all crimes committed) and attempted murder (33 per cent). Even more disturbingly, 53 per cent of convicted murderers were under 26 years old. At the time, poorly educated and heavily armed teenage gangs were able to operate with impunity, robbing vehicles along Albania's roads in broad daylight and, for much of 1997, making travel impossible in some parts of the country without an armed escort from the peace-keeping force. For many of these teenagers who had little prospect of employment or any sort of future, the ability to get rich quick and the excitement of engaging in adventurous and spectacular behaviour without fear of punishment were too much to resist. Eight thousand people have been injured by guns since 1997.

Although by the time the peace-keeping force left Albania in late 1997 some law and order had been restored, even today some roads in the country must be travelled with the utmost caution. Some areas have seen an alarming rise in banditry in recent months, and in much of the northeast, law and order are as good as absent. The situation has not been helped by the presence of heavily armed Kosovo Liberation Army (KLA) guerrillas, launching raids against Serbian forces in neighbouring Kosovo from northeastern Albania. Furthermore, the heavily armed north remains practically impossible to control because of its general isolation and poor transport infrastructure.

▼ *Teenagers handle guns before they are given up as part of a decommissioning exercise in central Albania.*

The arrival, and consequent departure, of more than half a million Kosovo Albanian refugees in the space of six months from March 1999 added to the instability in the north of the country. As thousands of distraught and traumatised refugees poured across the border, a massive aid effort was set in motion to help Albania deal with the worst humanitarian crisis in its history. The presence of hundreds of aid workers and NATO troops involved in the relief effort helped to ensure some order and relieve

Small arms

The UNDP and the Albanian Government have recently launched an arms recovery programme in the District of Gramsh, which is home to 42,000 people and one of the largest small-arms factories in Albania. Since March 1997, 600 people have been injured by guns in Gramsh; 57 were killed, almost half of them children. So far the police have managed to retrieve 5,000 guns. In this programme, villagers select infrastructure projects that they wish to see completed, in return for handing over their arms. In addition to the arms recovery programme, a nation-wide advocacy campaign against guns was launched through local NGOs.

In January 1999, a voluntary arms collection took place in the village of Tunjë. As villagers gathered, one of them was hopeful: 'I think most people will hand in their guns. The Government has promised to pave the road and put in a telephone line in return.' But most others were doubtful: 'We will give up some of our guns, but not all of them. I don't believe that they will build the road. The Government promised to build one before and they didn't—why should they do so now?' Some people compared the occasion to Communist initiatives: 'We were the first village in Albania to hand over our animals voluntarily to the co-operatives, and look where that got us. Now we are the first to hand in our guns—I hope we get something out of it this time.'

One villager was suspicious of the government's intentions: 'They promised they would bring us a transformer today, but look in their trucks—there is nothing. Once again, the government promises but doesn't deliver. We give up our guns in good faith, and then they forget their promises. Besides, we don't know what the government is doing with these guns. A lot of the police are ex-SIGURIMI, and I don't trust them. If we give up these guns but don't see them physically destroyed, how do we know that they won't be used against us? We don't trust the state, and we feel we have some power over them by keeping these guns.'

The distrust of state institutions goes deep: 'The politicians and the police just get fatter and richer and we get poorer. We have some power now that we didn't have before and we mean to make the government accountable for its promises.'

the burden on one of Albania's poorest, most isolated regions. But although most of the refugees returned to Kosovo when the war ended in July 1999, continued instability in Kosovo has not helped to lessen the problem of organised crime in Albania. Certain elements within the KLA have sought to use the power of the gun and their status as liberators to establish their control over political and economic activities; the NATO-led peace-keeping force in Kosovo has so far had relatively little success in curbing the excesses of various criminal groups operating both in Kosovo and out of northern Albania.

Despite the alarming statistics, particularly concerning the number of guns in civilian hands, it should be pointed out that many people armed themselves in response to the breakdown in law and order and a complete lack of personal security. Criminal elements in Albanian society are still the minority, and although most people possess a gun (in the rural areas almost every home has a Kalashnikov), most of these weapons are kept for self-defence only. Most Albanians want to hand in their guns but worry about their personal safety, given the continuing ineffectiveness of the police force. Many people also remain deeply suspicious of the government's motives. For many Albanians, the chaotic and misguided events of 1997 were their first genuine taste of freedom, as well as a final expression of frustration with the government's lack of accountability. They also a feel that some of the violence was politically motivated and could happen again. Any efforts to remove guns from everyday life in Albania must understand such concerns and give tangible reassurance to an apprehensive population, especially given the current confrontational political climate and the prospect of elections in late 2000.

▲ *Youngsters listening at a UN-sponsored pop concert organised as part of the national anti-gun campaign.*

Albanian identity and the Balkan factor

While Albania, unlike many of its Balkan neighbours, is the most ethnically homogeneous state in Europe, there are still divisions within it. The people of the north and south of the country consider themselves different, while almost 3 million Albanians live in the Serbian province of Kosovo and in the former Yugoslav Republic of Macedonia. Although all these groups consider themselves to be Albanian and speak the same language, different dialects and patterns of development have helped to create a very diverse Albanian identity. The Greek Albanian minority in the south and Roma communities enrich the cultural diversity, but also pose a challenge for achieving legal and social equality in Albania. The outbreak of war in Kosovo led to the issue of identity playing a much greater role in daily life in Albania than before.

North and south

The southern and central regions of modern-day Albania have always been seen as the most progressive and developed parts of the country. Profiting from access to the sea and being criss-crossed by several important trade routes, the southern half of the country has consistently developed most quickly, both economically and socially. Communist rule enforced this regional bias, as much of the partisan army that brought Hoxha and the Communists to power came from the south. Hoxha himself was from Gjirokastër, and his regime always weighted public spending and infrastructure development towards the south. As a result, life has been easier and more prosperous in the south, and this prosperity accounts for the greater openness and more liberal cultural attitudes to be found in Tiranë and to the south.

▼ People who live in rural areas, like Lula Stani and her children, need to share in Albania's economic recovery.

The north does not share the same sense of prosperity. It has always been isolated from the rest of the country: in Skenderbeg's time, it provided the most significant resistance to the advances of the Ottoman Empire.

▲ *People in Albania's northern mountains have kept to their traditions.*

Even under Ottoman rule from 1500 to 1912, large areas of the north used the inaccessibility of the rugged mountainous terrain to preserve their traditional customs. Most notable was the development of the Kanun of Lek Dukagjine, the north's own common law. Lek Dukagjine was a notable tribal chieftain in the fifteenth century who managed to document and codify the northern system of tribal law. This complex set of laws in this codex came to govern every aspect of social life in the north, and the Kanun is still very much alive today. In spite of its more regrettable aspects, such as the severe restriction of freedom for women and the concept of blood feuds, many communities in the north have clung to the Kanun as they struggle to make sense of the void left behind by the end of communism. The area's deprivation under communism, and its continuing isolation, have aggravated the endemic poverty in the region and are the two most important factors contributing to the massive migration to towns like Shkodër and shantytowns like Kamza in Tiranë.

'I don't think the villages will ever be empty': Nikol's story

Nikol Pietr comes from the village of Toplanë in Shllak Commune, which is surrounded by high mountains and has a spectacular view of the River Drin. It has no road, and the only way to get to the nearest town, Shkodër, is by boat and then by bus. Life in Shllak is still governed by the Kanun and its conservative traditions. Although life is hard in the village, Nikol is keen to stay. 'Life is better now than ten years ago, when there were 28 people in my family and we all had to live in the same house. In the past eight years we have been able to expand our houses: now everyone has his or her own bed.'

However, safety has declined as people have used traditional law to gain power and wealth. Nikol regrets this: 'It is very sad because it gives us a bad image and makes people in the rest of the country look down on us, despite the fact that we are a proud people with many noble traditions and customs.' Like most northerners, Nikol keeps guns for his own protection; but he has not had to make use of them: 'Fortunately, my family has always been peaceful and we have no quarrels with anyone. For me there are only two or three bad families in Toplanë. I try to work with everyone rather than hide from them. You just have to be firm and gain their respect. If they know you are not to be messed with and will not change your principles then they will leave you alone. Nevertheless, although I feel safe during the day, I never take the same path twice at night. We have a saying that "the night has no faith".'

Nikol worries about the amount of guns in currency. 'Only the state should have guns. In the old days, when we used to have one or two guns, we would fire them for sounding an alarm. Recently, there was a fire in our village and I used my gun to sound the alarm. Because guns are used for all the wrong reasons now, nobody came—they were afraid. It is sad that there is no more trust in the village. We must see ourselves as a community like we used to, or we won't survive. I think community spirit still exists more up here than in the south. However, I don't know for how much longer it can survive with all these guns and the violence.'

▲ Nikol Pietr with his wife, children, and their grandfather.

It is difficult to make a living in Toplanë: 'I get a small salary as the village electrician and I repair people's tools. I am able to feed my family from my land even though the land is poor. It would be better if I could get more manure for fertiliser, but it is difficult to keep cows here in the mountains. Even though people in the village need tools they often don't have money to pay for them or the repairs I can make.'

Like everyone, Nikol has considered moving to Shkodër; while he reckons that he cannot afford the move, a stronger motivation for staying in Toplanë is his sense of belonging there. 'If I were to move to the town I would have to create new friends, whereas here I know everybody. The best families are staying here in the village. The bad families tend to go to Shkodër because they have got some money illegally, which is why I don't really like Shkodër. I don't think the villages will ever be empty like some people are saying. For people here, the village and the mountains are their identity, and this sense of identity with your home is much stronger here than in the south. For us the mountains have an almost holy significance. The good people in the villages still feel this very strongly.

'Every village, just like anywhere else, has some bad people who don't feel this sense of attachment and community. They simply use the traditions of the north to further their own gains through violence and intimidation, giving the culture of the north a bad name; sadly, this is what the rest of the country sees of us. I try to remain true to my principles and treat everyone with fairness and respect. I want to give my children a good example and make them proud of this place. I do want them to be educated though, and perhaps I will have to leave Toplanë because of this. However, I will keep my place here to come back to. It is beautiful and clean here, and I am at peace in this place.'

Kosovo

In the post-communist period, many Kosovar Albanians were able to travel to Albania for the first time. Despite the hardship they suffered under the Serbian system, they were shocked at the poverty and deprivation in Albania, as well as the huge cultural gulf that had opened between Kosovo and Albania. Before the repression of the Albanian majority in Kosovo in 1989, as Yugoslav citizens, Kosovar Albanians had enjoyed many freedoms and considerable prosperity compared to their kinspeople in Enver Hoxha's Albania. As a result, Kosovar Albanians aspire to independence rather than unification with Albania.

But despite these differences, many people in the north of Albania have distant relatives in Kosovo and feel strong sympathy for the plight of Albanians in Kosovo. Albania let in thousands of refugees, as well as allowing the KLA to operate from various bases in northeastern Albania. For many refugees, their time in Albania was a confusing experience. Life in the northeast, particularly during the bitterly cold winters, was too difficult, and most refugees have moved south to Durrës and Tiranë, where traditional feelings of cultural superiority made their integration into the community difficult.

Albania was ill-equipped to deal with the unprecedented number of refugees from Kosovo which began flooding across its borders in March 1999. While Albanians showed remarkable care and compassion for the refugees, Albania is a poor country, and its citizens are having to endure significant economic hardship themselves. There was a danger of Albanian resentment of the great international aid effort that primarily benefited the half a million Kosovar refugees, rather than the host population. With the end of the war in Kosovo and the return of the majority of refugees, this danger is reduced. However, the aid effort has moved to Kosovo with the refugees, leaving many important projects that would have benefited Albanians unfinished, and communities feel abandoned and once more forgotten by the rest of the world. As an Albanian expressed it, 'For the rest of the world, Albania is like a book with a flashy cover; everybody wants to read the first chapter, but then loses interest and never wants to finish it.'

▼ *Faz Berisha, who wants to live in a place where her children can be safe and have a future.*

At the time of these interviews in January 1999 there were 5,000 refugees from Kosovo in Durrës. Life is difficult for them: for example, they have to find private accommodation which is expensive and often of poor quality. Local people's attitudes towards them ranged from indifference to small acts of kindness, but also outright hostility. Faz Berisha and her family from the village of Decan in Kosovo have been in Durrës for four months. 'Life here for us is expensive, and the conditions are very primitive. All my family has come here, but my brother's family is still in Kosovo. It is difficult to get news from them and know if they are all still alive. We are very worried since the massacres at Racak.' Faz lays responsibility for the conflict in Kosovo at the West's door: 'They drew the borders and thus separated us in 1912. We watched Bosnia on our television screens, and we have always lived with the fear that the same thing would happen to us.'

Some parents have decided to send their children to school in Durrës, but it is hard for the children to fit in. Because many Kosovar Albanians are just waiting to leave Albania, they are reluctant to get their children settled into school. Faz is not sure what to do. 'My daughter is ten years old and she should be in school. In Kosovo, she was a very bright student. I just want to go home to Kosovo. If I can't go home I would like to go to Germany, where my husband has worked for 28 years. I had imagined Albania to be a better place than it actually is. Albanians are used to it, but it is difficult for us. Everybody should be able to live in his or her own home. We should be one nation and have the right to be together, but I think it will take a long time for attitudes and circumstances to change.'

Perhaps Faz and her family have since returned to Kosovo and started rebuilding their lives; and perhaps the NATO-led intervention in Kosovo will secure peace in the province, in the long term encouraging the Serb and Albanian communities to negotiate a sustainable solution that will safeguard the rights of all people in Kosovo.

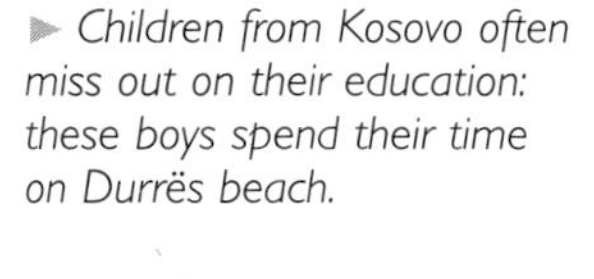

► Children from Kosovo often miss out on their education: these boys spend their time on Durrës beach.

Conclusion: the need for choice and opportunity

Thousands of Albanians are working hard to rebuild their country, despite enormous obstacles. While researching this book, many Albanians I spoke to were anxious to know how their country would be portrayed. Albanians are upset that Western media tend to focus on their problems, rather than profile the efforts of the many people who are working for change. They are very much aware of their country's negative reputation abroad, and its demoralising effects: if the stereotype of '"that crazy little country in the Balkans" gets fed back to our own media, it reinforces people's negative view of the situation here and the feeling that everything is hopeless.'

> 'It is important that the rest of the world sees that we are trying. We are afraid, but we must overcome this and make the world realise that we are not all criminals with guns.'
>
> *Afroviti Gushto, Reflexione, Pogradec.*

As Albania continues its long and painful transition to democracy, the international community must take a much greater interest in the country. Western governments must also be much more supportive of Albanians' demands for accountability from their new government than they have been in the past. Although such policies will need to respect Albania's sovereignty, the lack of effective international pressure in the past allowed some of the excesses of the Berisha government. Without concrete support from Western countries for a genuine and pluralistic democracy in Albania, this key strategic Balkan country will not be able to create long-term political, economic and social stability. Western governments must not regard Albania and its government merely as tools for servicing wider regional security concerns, with little regard for human rights or genuine economic and social development.

A more balanced view of Albania in other countries would encourage younger people, such as these students in Tiranë, to envisage a future in Albania.

European governments and the USA must also play an influential role in ensuring that the country's first constitution that genuinely enshrines democratic principles is adhered to and implemented by its politicians. As an old man in Pogradec told me: 'Democracy here still exists on paper only. I have my freedom of speech, but I am like a parrot—I talk, but nobody listens to me.'

Indications however, are positive, and Albanians are emerging from the chaos of 1997 and the failure of the country's first experiment with democracy wiser and determined to make a fresh start. The post–1997 government made a promising start, and Western support, particularly in the run-up to the 2000 elections, must ensure that accountability is maintained and that the government keeps its promises. More funding is being targeted towards NGOs and the civil society sector, as the government realises that NGOs must be seen as effective partners, rather than opponents. The country's post-communist constitution of 1998 is in place, enshrining a broad spectrum of rights and freedoms for all Albanians. Local community initiatives are becoming more common outside Tiranë; individuals like those interviewed for this book are being recognised in their communities and serving as useful role models in a society that had its social values and reference systems turned upside down.

This is not to say that the path ahead will be easy. The continuing problem of law and order, and an armed population, will still take a long time to resolve. The huge amounts of Western aid given to Albania to date were allocated with little attempt to understand the needs and views of ordinary people in Albania, and channelled through governments which were completely out of touch with the concerns and aspirations of the population. As a result, Albanians themselves have not been much involved in Albania's development since 1992. This has left people continually frustrated with the state and its institutions. Without involvement in their own country's development, it is difficult for people to feel a sense of ownership of the new Albania, or any sense of community and collective responsibility. Attitudes such as 'winner takes all' and 'live for today—who knows what tomorrow might bring' have been predominant in Albanian society.

▼ Sceptical about what the future holds…

However, there are numerous examples, primarily supported by local and foreign NGOs, where project beneficiaries have been painstakingly involved in every aspect of a project's development. It took a long time for results to materialise, as people came to terms with the novelty of being listened to and exercising their opinions. Yet during the turmoil of 1997, it was these types of project that escaped unscathed, or in some cases were valiantly defended by the beneficiaries themselves, while many state-run and donor-funded projects were looted or destroyed. People felt that they had built these projects themselves, based on their own needs and concerns. It is this process of actively involving Albanians from all walks of life in the development debate that will be key in helping Albania find its

Apart from political and economic progress, Albanians need to nourish a sense of community and co-operation.

new identity and make its way into the new millennium with confidence. This will take serious commitment from both the Albanian Government and European donors. Assistance to Albania must be targeted with popular participation in mind, rather than with the short-term goal of safeguarding internal stability.

As an Albanian friend of mine told me once: 'Put three Albanians in a room, and you will find that there are six different opinions. To you, this may seem crazy, but remember that we have not been allowed to have an opinion until now. These are exciting times for us: we have a lot of options to choose from, and no experience of how to make such choices. This will come with time, but you must let us have the space to make these decisions and achieve consent. This will not happen overnight.' It is hoped that their Government and the rest of the world will grant the people of Albania this space in the years to come.

The human tragedy that unfolded in Kosovo in 1999 once more thrust Albania onto the world stage. Albanians' courageous response to this crisis, along with their continuing efforts to resolve their own significant economic, social, and political difficulties, will need more support now than ever. This time, Albanians will need to see beyond the immediate effects of this latest crisis and receive the support they need, both from their own Government and those in the West, to ensure that the lessons of the past ten years are used to build a firm foundation for the future.

Neil Olsen

Dates and events

2000 BC
Emergence of Illyrian culture in Balkan peninsula.

800-600 BC
Greeks establish colonies in peninsula.

4th century BC
Height of Illyrian kingdom. Invasions by Philip of Macedonia and Alexander the Great.

168 BC
Roman Empire controls Illyrian territory.

4th to 7th century AD
Former Illyrian territory becomes part of the Byzantine Empire. Invasions by Visigoths, Ostrogoths, Huns, Serbs and Croats.

1054
Christian church splits into Catholic and Orthodox denominations.

9th to 14th century
Albanian territory dominated by Bulgarians, Italians, Serbs, Turks.

▲ *A defaced fresco at Ardinicë monastery.*

1430
Ottoman Empire establishes control.

1443-68
Skenderbeg defeats Ottoman army and unites Albanian rulers. After his death, the Ottoman Empire re-establishes rule.

1878
Albanian League founded; its goals include unification of Albanian territories and cultural emancipation.

1910-12
Armed struggle to achieve democratic reform and autonomy. Vlorë Congress declares independence after allied Greek, Serbian and Montenegrin forces declare war on Turkey.

1912
Balkan allies defeat Turkey. Western European 'great powers' accept Albanian independence but cede large territories to Serbia and Greece.

1914–18
Chaos as various Western European and Balkan armies invade Albania.

1920
National congress held in Lushnjë; progressive government under Fan Noli, opposed by conservative group led by Ahmet Bey Zogu.

1925–39
Zogu overthrows Noli's liberal government and rules as president and king.

1939–45
Albania occupied by Italian and German armies. Communist groups form resistance and gain control in 1944; their leader is Enver Hoxha.

1946

Albania declared the People's Republic of Albania, ruled by Hoxha's Party of Labour. Economic and diplomatic ties with Yugoslavia (until 1948), the Soviet Union (until 1960), and China (until 1978).

1967

Religious worship is banned and all mosques and churches closed.

1985

Enver Hoxha dies.

1990–91

Hoxha's successor Ramiz Alia allows independent political parties. Occupations of foreign embassies by about 5,000 people. Pro-democracy demonstrations in Tiranë.

1992

Democratic Party led by Sali Berisha wins elections.

1993–97

Increasing government authoritarianism and corruption.

1997

March: Widespread anarchy, rioting and looting of army weapons stores following collapse of pyramid investment schemes. Transitional government of Fatos Nano and his Socialist Party takes over from Berisha.
April: Arrival of multinational peace-keeping force.
May: Elections. Socialists gain power under President Medani and Prime Minister Nano.
July–August: Departure of peace-keeping force.

1998

Nano resigns under pressure and Pandeli Majko becomes Prime Minister. Sali Berisha regains leadership of the DP.

December 1999

Pandeli Majko resigns as Prime Minister.

January 2000

Fatos Nano returns as Prime Minister. Elections scheduled for later in the year.

► *Mother Albania, one of the few statues from communist times that was left standing in 1990–91.*

Facts and figures

Land area

28,750 km^2

Population

3.4m (1998)

Annual average growth rate: 2.01 per cent per annum (1996)

46 per cent (1997) of Albanians live in urban areas

Currency

Lek (1 Lek = 100 quintars)
141 Lek = US$1 (January 2000)

Education

Compulsory school enrolment (8 grades): 100 per cent; boys 51.7 per cent, girls 48.3 per cent (1998)

Students going on to high school: 61 per cent (1997)

Adult literacy: 91.8 per cent (1989)

Spending on education as percentage of GNP: 11 per cent (1997)

Average life expectancy

68.5 years for men, 74.3 years for women (1995)

Health

Infant mortality rate: 43.3 per 1000 births (1997)

Maternal mortality rate:

25.2 per 100,000 live births (1992)

Health expenditure as percentage of GNP

6 per cent (1997)

Physicians per 10,000 people:

18.1 (1994)

Health units per 10,000 people:

85.3 (1994)

Access to safe water

56.4 per cent (1989)

Access to sanitation

96.6 per cent (1989)

Gross National Product

US$3,407m (1998)
US$1,002 US$ per capita (1998)
Average annual growth (1998): 8 per cent
Average annual growth (1997): -7 per cent

Structure of Gross Domestic Product (1997)

Agriculture: 56.0 per cent
Industry: 12.4 per cent
Construction: 11.2 per cent
Transport: 2.7 per cent
Others: 17.6 per cent

Inflation

20.7 per cent (1998)

Current account balance

US$ -65.1 million (1998)
US$ -272.1 million (1997)

External debt

US$ 270 million (1997)

Main foreign donors (1997)

EU: 35 per cent
Italy: 14 per cent
World Bank: 13 per cent
USA: 10 per cent
Germany: 10 per cent

Sources: UNDP Human Development Reports 1995, 1996, 1998, Economist Intelligence Unit

Sources and further reading

Balkan politics

Kosovo: Oppression of Ethnic Albanians, Urgent Issues Paper (London: The Minority Rights Group, 1992)

Minorities in the Balkans, Report No.82 (London: The Minority Rights Group, 1989)

James Pettifer and Hugh Poulton The Southern Balkans (London: The Minority Rights Group (Greece), 1994)

General interest

http://reenic.utexas.edu/reenic/Countries/Albania/albania.html#Subjects

International Journal of Albanian Studies c/o Shinasi A. Rama, Department of Political Science, Columbia University, New York, NY 10027, USA

www.albania.co.uk

www.albanian.com

www.middlebury.edu/~como/albania.shtml

History

Amnesty International Albania: Political Imprisonment and the law (London: Amnesty International, 1984)

Bill Hamilton and Bhasker Solanki Albania: Who Cares? (London: Grantham, 1992)

John Wilkes The Illyrians (Oxford: Blackwell, 1992)

Literature and culture

Robert Elsie History of Albanian Literature (New York: University Presses of California, Columbia and Princeton, 1995)

Ismail Kadare Broken April (London: Saqi Press, 1990)
The General of the Dead Army (London: Quartet Books, 1986)

http://studweb.studserv.uni-stuttgart.de/studweb/users/ger/ger10999/english/english.html

Politics and development

EIU Country Report Albania (Economist Intelligence Unit, 2000)

Nicholas Panno 'The Process of Democratisation in Albania', in Karen Dawisha and Bruce Parrott (eds.) Politics, Power and the Struggle for Democracy in Southeast Europe (Cambridge University Press, 1997)

Miranda Vickers Albania: From Anarchy to a Balkan Identity (C Hurst & Co, 1997)

www.undp.org/rbec/nhdr/1996/summary/albania.htm

www.unhcr.ch/world/euro/albania.htm

www.washingtonpost.com/wp-srv/inatl/longterm/worldref/country/albania.htm

www.worldwidenews.com/albania.htm

Travel

Robert Carver The Accursed Mountains (London: Flamingo, 1999)

James Pettifer Blue Guide: Albania (London: A&C Black and New York: WW Norton, 1994)

Oxfam in Albania

Oxfam GB has been working in Albania since 1992, at first distributing winter clothing in the north of the country as well as providing initial support to a group of fledgling local NGOs.

In 1993 Oxfam established a permanent presence in Albania, in order to work on issues of rural poverty, gender equality, disability, and NGO development. A major rural development programme in the Commune of Shllak in Shkodër District, one of the country's poorest and most isolated areas, started in 1994. Self-help projects include water supply and income-generating activities. Despite the cultural difficulties in this very traditional area, Oxfam has also worked directly with women. A rural resource and training centre serving both lowland and highland farmers has been set up.

In 1994 Oxfam in Albania set up the country's first resource centre for people with disabilities. The project established the first production facility for wheelchairs: to date, more than 200 individually designed wheelchairs have been produced and distributed. In addition, the project has provided active rehabilitation camps and independent living skills training. In 1997, the resource centre became independent from Oxfam and is now a well-established, high-profile local NGO, the Albanian Disability Rights Foundation (ADREF).

Oxfam has also played a significant role in supporting Albanian women's organisations like Reflexione. It helped in establishing the LINEA counselling centre in Shkodër, which offers assistance and support to women on issues of domestic violence.

Most recently, Oxfam in Albania has developed a public awareness campaign on arms control with the UNDP. Oxfam also remains very active in the area of emergency preparedness and worked with UNHCR in responding to the Kosovo refugee crisis in 1998 and 1999.

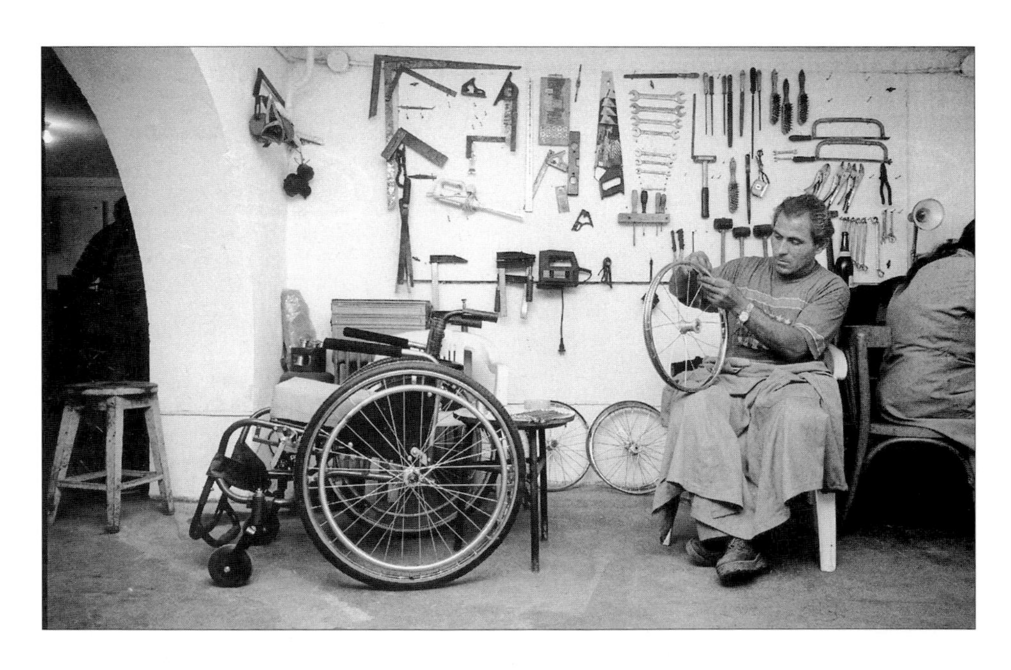

At the ADREF workshop, which employs wheelchair users, each wheelchair is custom-made.

Index

abduction 40, 43–4
abortion 49
ADREF 53–4, 61, 86
agriculture 12
  co-operatives 21–2, 35
  industrial pollution 68-9
  seasonal employment 38–9
  small-scale 32–3, 35, 36, 56
Albania, image in foreign media 9, 38, 79, 80
Albania, north 13, 16, 35, 58–9, 71, 74–6
Alia, Ramiz 23, 83
authoritarianism 9, 24, 28–9

Balkan politics 8–9, 13–14, 17, 74, 79
Ballsh 65, 68–9
banditry 26, 40, 71, 73
  see also abduction, mafia
Berisha, Sali 13–14, 23–4, 25, 26, 28–9, 30, 83
blood feuds 16, 26, 59, 71, 75
border issues 13–14, 18, 37–9, 77
Bosnian war 34–5
Byzantine Empire 12, 82

cars 34, 48–9, 67
censorship 24, 27, 62
central planning 30-1
China 19, 30, 31
civil society 7, 80
civilians, armed 25–6, 70, 72, 73, 80
comedy festivals 15–6
communist state
  arts subsidies 15
  disabilities 60–1
  divorce 57–8
  education 42
  health care 47–8, 50
  overthrow 6–7, 23, 27–8
  political prisoners 21–2
  secret police 20, 21, 24, 72
  see also SIGURIMI
  southern/central bias 74
  see also Hoxha

constitutions 18, 25, 58–9, 79–80
contraception 49
corruption 9, 21, 24
counselling 54, 56, 57, 58, 86
credit rationing 33
crime 43, 44, 70, 71, 73
culture 9–10, 14–16, 62–4
  traditional 5-6, 7, 15–16, 58–9, 75

deforestation 66
democracy 6–7, 26, 41, 79–81, 83
  inexperience 7, 21, 22, 29, 52
  parliamentary 23–4
  women's status 55
Democratic Party 23–4, 26, 27, 29, 83
disability 53–4, 60–4, 86
dissent 20, 23, 24, 29
divorce 57–8
doctors 48–9, 51
Durrës 35, 77

economic crisis 23–4, 30, 37, 49
economic reform 23, 25, 30–3, 50
economy 8–9, 30–6, 48–9, 84
  see also emigration
education 42–6, 50–1, 77–8, 84
Elbasan steelworks 31–2, 65
emigration 28, 32, 34, 37–41, 64
  doctors 51
  education 43
  effects 31, 45–6
  gender 56
  NGOs 38
  see also migrant workers, young people
environmental pollution 65–9
European powers' involvement 6, 8–9, 18, 24, 79, 79–82
ethnicity 14, 74

foreign domination 6–9, 17, 82

gender factors 43–4, 49, 55–9
geography 11–12, 84
Gjirokastër 13, 15, 41, 74

Greece
  Albanians 31, 37, 38, 39–40, 45
  seasonal employment 34, 39
Greek-speaking Albanians 14, 40–1, 74

health care 33, 47–51, 84
  infant mortality 47–8, 84
history 5–7, 12–13, 17–20, 82–3
Hoxha, Enver 5, 19–20, 23, 74, 82–3
  education 42
  economy 31
  international ties 19, 83
  oppression 6–7, 19–22, 29, 37
  statue toppled 5, 28
human-rights abuses 24

identity, Albanian 7, 74–8
IMF 24, 48
independence 18, 82
industrial pollution 65–6, 68–9
international aid 8, 35, 54, 71, 73, 79, 80–1, 84
investment 24–5, 35–6
Italian invasion 5, 18, 19, 82
Italy, Albanians 31, 37, 38

Kanun of Lek Dukagjine 16, 75
Korçë 44, 49–51
Korçë District Hospital 50-1
Kosovo 8, 77–8, 81
Kosovo Albanian refugees 8, 13, 37, 71, 73, 77–8, 86
Kosovo Liberation Army 8, 71, 73, 77

land conflict 70–1
languages 13–14, 45
law and order 20, 25, 31–2, 70–3, 80
life expectancy 47–8, 49, 84
LINEA 56, 57, 58, 86
literacy 42
  see also education
literature 16, 62–4
looting 25, 31, 39, 42, 70, 80

mafia 26, 40, 70
Majko, Pandeli 25, 26, 83
Medani, Rexhep 25, 26, 83
media 15–16, 24, 26, 27, 37, 62
migrant workers 30, 31, 34, 37, 38, 39–40
  see also emigration
Mussolini, Benito 19

Nano, Fatos 23, 25, 26, 83
NATO 71, 73, 78, 83
NGOs 52–4, 86
  crime 43
  disability 61
  emigration 38
  environmental issues 67, 68
  funding 54, 80
  north Albania 35
  small-scale farmers 36
  women's groups 55, 59
Noli, Fan 18, 82

oil fields 66, 68–9
Ottoman Empire 6, 12, 17, 82

poetry 16, 62–4
police 70, 73
  see also SIGURIMI
political prisoners 20–2
politics 9–10
  authoritarianism 9, 24, 28–9
  borders 13–14, 18, 37–9, 77
  coalition 23, 25
  corruption 9, 21, 24
  elections 23-4, 79–80, 83
  parties 23–4, 25, 26, 27, 29
  public attitudes 9-10, 72
pollution 31, 65–9
population 30
poverty 34–6, 44–5
privatisation 31-2
prostitution 43, 56–7, 63
public attitudes 9–10, 67, 72
public transport 39, 44
pyramid investment schemes
  24–5, 35–6

Qemali, Ismail 18

radio 62
Reflexione 56, 58–9, 80, 86
religion 12–13, 82–3
remittances 30
road network 31
Roma minority 14
Romania 28, 45
rural-urban migration 35, 75
rural areas 33, 34
  education 42
  health care 48–9
  poverty 34–6
  prostitution 57
  women's status 57, 58, 59

sanitation 47, 49, 84
seasonal employment 34, 39
security 9, 41
  abduction 43–4
  gender 40, 43–4, 56
  peace-keeping forces 25, 73
  private industry 32
  weapons 73, 75–6
Serbia 82
  see also Kosovo
shanty-towns 35, 75
Shkodër 34, 35–6, 58
SIGURIMI 20, 21, 24, 72
Skenderbeg, Gjergj Kastrioti
  5, 17, 82
social unrest 25, 36, 49-50, 52
Socialist Party 25, 26, 83
soil erosion 66
Stalinism 19, 30
student protest 23, 27-8, 40

teachers 22, 42, 43, 46
Tiranë 5–6, 28, 35
  shantytowns 35, 75
  Tiranë University 27, 43

UN peace-keeping 8
UNDP 36, 37–8, 43, 71, 72, 86
unemployment 28, 30, 31, 35–6, 55
UNESCO 12–13
UNHCR 86
universities 27, 40–1, 43

vaccination 47–8
violence, domestic 57–8, 59
virginesh 59
volunteerism 52
Voskopojë 42–5

Yugoslavia 19
  see also Kosovo

water supplies 47, 49, 84
weaponry 25–6, 70, 72, 73, 75–6, 80
welfare allowance 34, 61, 62
wheelchairs 61, 62, 64, 86
women
  counselling 54, 56-8, 86
  divorce 57–8
  family planning 49
  Kanun 75
  maternal mortality 48, 84
  rural areas 57, 58, 59
  traditions 16
  violence against 57–8, 59
  see also culture, gender factors
Women's Centre 52, 58
women's movement 52, 53, 55–9
work permits 39–40
World Bank 24, 48

Yugoslavia 9, 19, 83
  see also Kosovo
Younger generation 27–9, 40–1

Zogu, Ahmet 18, 82